Dad's Guide to Pregnancy

2nd Australian Edition

by Dr Justin Coulson

T0366648

for
dummies®
A Wiley Brand

Dad's Guide to Pregnancy For Dummies®, 2nd Australian Edition

Published by
John Wiley & Sons, Australia Ltd
42 McDougall Street
Milton, Qld 4064
www.dummies.com

Copyright © 2022 John Wiley & Sons Australia, Ltd

The moral rights of the author have been asserted.

Additional material authored by Stefan Korn, Scott Lancaster, Eric Mooij, Directors, DIY Father

ISBN: 978-1-119-91031-2

A catalogue record for this book is available from the National Library of Australia

Cover image: © 9dream studio/Shutterstock

Typeset by Straive

Contents at a Glance

Table of Contents

Introduction

The expression 'useless as a chocolate teacup' comes to mind when describing what many fathers in the past felt about their involvement during labour and when caring for newborns. Fathers historically have taken a passive role during pregnancy, going about their lives mostly as normal (and wondering what the rules are about pregnancy and intimacy). They've offered a shoulder rub to their partner during childbirth. And when it came to looking after babies, history is replete with examples of men avoiding the multiple night-time wakings, and feigning strategic incompetence when nappies needed changing.

But that was then. These days, an increasing number of guys now want a piece of the baby action, and are rolling up their sleeves to muck in with everything that needs doing — from active involvement in labour to cutting the cord through to nappy changes (although probably not the poo explosions), along with the fun of baby baths and tummy time.

The number of stay-at-home dads (SAHDs) is rising in almost all developed countries — a sure sign that the parenting world is changing and that staying home looking after the kids is no longer a reason to hand in your man card. In fact, SAHDs are leading the way for all other dads to show the world how brilliant dads can be at looking after babies and children.

Parental leave in workplaces is changing too. Corporations are recognising that not just mum needs time off when a baby is born. The organisational trend is towards parental leave for fathers so they can support their partner, bond with their baby, and savour the precious early moments of parenting. And parental leave for dads is happening more and more, even in sectors where the alpha male and his over-the-top commitment to the company have historically dominated. (I'm looking at you, financial sector.)

Moreover, many nations, particularly Holland, Sweden and Finland, actively encourage parents to work a four-day week. Time with family is prized and honoured. Government policy encourages it, and for good reason.

Countless studies by fatherhood institutes around the world show strong scientific evidence for the positive difference a dad makes in the lives of his children. Unfortunately, many of the challenges and difficulties our children experience are linked to absent, uninvolved or unsafe fathers. And while it's true that children raised by single mums can — and do — thrive (because their mothers are phenomenal), there is little doubt that fathers count. In comparison to children raised without the positive presence of a dad in their lives, kids raised by a positive, active, involved and safe dad have an increased likelihood of doing better at self-regulation, delayed gratification, emotional management, social relationships, academic achievement, avoiding unsafe, unhealthy behaviours as teens — the list goes on. Oh yeah, and they're happier and more satisfied with life. Measurably.

The journey of being a dad starts way back at the very beginning, even before conception. It starts with the way you love your partner, the mum of your soon-to-be child. The great news is that more dads are keen to be a positive, active, involved member of the family, and society's conditions are ripe for helping us make it happen.

About This Book

With *Dad's Guide to Pregnancy For Dummies*, I'm doing my bit to help every new dad or dad-to-be start his journey to healthy, safe, active fatherhood. In this book, I focus specifically on pregnancy from a male perspective. The great news is being a healthy, safe, active dad isn't difficult. Dads can do everything mums do except giving birth and breastfeeding. So if you're worried about becoming a dad, relax, read on and know that everyday blokes make fantastic dads.

I'm thrilled to be able to serve as your guide to dadhood. Since 2012, my organisation — Dr Justin Coulson's Happy Families — has developed into one of the most recognised organisations promoting, well, happy families — and involved fatherhood — in Australia and New Zealand. In *Dad's Guide to Pregnancy For Dummies*, 2nd edition, I share what the very best science has taught us about how you can be involved in your children's lives for better — and how doing so can build a happier life for your child, and for you.

I've spent years talking to hundreds of thousands of parents about this stuff. And I've also had plenty of practice. My wife and I have six of our own kids, so I've got the miles in the legs. I'm race fit and ready to share the research and the practice to make this gig hum for you. And what all of this means is that you can find all you need to know in one place (this book), and don't need to waste time reading lots of leaflets or browsing through hundreds of websites trying to get reliable and practical information from a male perspective. I've packed these pages with plenty of useful information so you can become the best father you can be.

So, why this book? The reasons include the following:

>> The Baby Boomer (1950s) approach to having children cast a long shadow into the way we approach modern parenting, but things have changed. Modern dads want to be involved and they want to find out for themselves what they need to know to look after a newborn baby.

>> Your kids, your family and our world need strong dads. Fathers have been somewhat absent from childcare and upbringing due to work, family situation or a limited understanding of the role of a father. It's about time we changed that.

>> You may find even approaching the topic of pregnancy and babies hard.

>> You may be missing out on the best moments of your life if you feel you don't know what to do with (newborn) babies.

>> You have everything you need to be a fantastic dad, but you just don't know it yet. Or perhaps you lack a bit of confidence to demonstrate your dad skills. This book will help.

>> Your baby and partner are likely to really appreciate all the cool things you know and are able to do when you've read this book.

>> By being a positive, healthy, active dad right from the beginning, you make the most significant contribution to your child's life you could ever make — it beats any expensive present, university savings account or inheritance fund your child may receive.

Foolish Assumptions

I assume that you're reading this book because you've just been told that you're going to be a dad soon or you've decided it's about time you became one. You may also have been told by your partner to 'skill up' and read about pregnancy and parenting so she doesn't have to do all the work around the baby. Good — because you don't want that anyway. Today's dads can do everything that mums do except giving birth and breastfeeding.

I assume you're somewhat puzzled by the prospects of becoming a dad and would like an easy and comprehensive guide. This book is for you if you're

>> Freaked out about becoming a dad

>> Concerned about your lack of knowledge and experience around all things babies

>> Three months into your partner's pregnancy and feel like it's all getting a bit too complicated

>> Looking for an alternative to being told everything you need to know about babies by your partner

>> On your way to the delivery suite and have missed all the ante-natal classes

I also assume you haven't had much exposure to or experience with pregnant women and newborn babies up to now.

Although I hope you read every word I've written, I understand your life is busy and you want to read only the need-to-know info. You can safely skip the sidebars, which are shaded grey boxes containing text. These provide supporting or entertaining information that isn't critical to your understanding of the topic.

Throughout this book, I give you the website addresses of a number of dedicated parenting or fatherhood sites where you can find more information on some of the topics discussed, such as buying sensible baby gear and toys, newborn baby care, illnesses and special conditions, as well as male postnatal depression. Although you don't have to go to these websites, having a browse through them is worthwhile.

Icons Used in This Book

Icons are those little pictures you see sprinkled in the margins throughout this book. Here's what they mean.

CHECK
THE NET

The internet is a wonderful place to access information on being a great dad. This icon highlights some helpful sites for you to check out.

REMEMBER

This icon denotes critical information that you really need to take away with you. Considering the state of my own overcrowded brain, I wouldn't ask you to remember anything unless the information was really important.

TIP

This bullseye alerts you to on-target advice, insights or recommendations that I've picked up over the years.

WARNING

This icon serves as a warning — telling you to avoid something that's potentially harmful. Take heed!

Where to Go from Here

You choose what happens next. This book is packed with information to help you at whatever state or stage you're at on your fatherhood journey. You can go directly to the topics of most interest to you, or you can start at the beginning and take it from there. With the information in *Dad's Guide to Pregnancy For Dummies*, 2nd edition, I'm confident that you're able to master any challenges your partner's pregnancy (or your new offspring) throws at you. Most importantly, this book helps you become a confident and competent dad, and have fun along the way.

1

From Here to Paternity: Getting Pregnant

Find out what being a dad is really all about — and what it isn't.

Understand being a dad doesn't start the day you meet your newborn child; instead, the process begins much sooner than that — in some cases, even from before your child is conceived.

Prepare for the hurdles you may face on the way to getting pregnant and meeting your baby.

Chapter **1**

Everything You Ever Wanted to Know . . .

f you've picked up this book, you're probably faced with one of the following scenarios:

» Your partner just told you she's pregnant

» Your partner has made it abundantly clear her biological clock is ticking and she really wants a baby now

» You've decided you're ready to be a father and want to put this plan into action

» You're being stalked by someone and are just pretending to read a book in a bookshop . . . put the book down, walk slowly away

Whatever your situation, you've come to the right place. Knowledge is power, and I've written *Dad's Guide to Pregnancy For*

Dummies to help dads-to-be find out more about this 'pregnancy thing', and outline everything you need to know about having a baby.

In this chapter, I run through some common myths about fatherhood, and how you can put some thought and planning into being a 21st-century dad. But first, let's focus on you. . .

Imaging the Dad You Want to Be

I'm going to use a fancy phrase here to set up a bit of a thought experiment. The phrase is 'temporal distancing', which basically means I'd like you to do a mental time-travel exercise. Psychologists highlight how temporal distancing (imagining a future state) helps us to get clear on who we really are and what we really value. So here goes. Insert your relevant time-travel pop-culture reference (for me it's *Back to the Future* and the flux capacitor), and let's pay a visit to the future.

Imagine yourself 20 to 30 years from now. You're sitting around the outdoor table. You've just enjoyed a tasty BBQ (sirloin steak cooked medium rare) and the grandkids are playing with some LEGO and other blocks on the floor. (Of course LEGO's still around!) And you're watching them with awe while you listen to your *adult children* chatting about how you were as a dad and how you raised them. How would you like your children to remember you? What stories are they telling? What do they remember about the way you responded when they made mistakes, got it wrong, laid into each other as only siblings can, and refused to do as they were told (as all kids will from time to time)? Do they remember you being on the sidelines of their games? Were you in the audience at their recitals or assemblies? Did your face light up when they walked into the room?

I know imagining life as a grandparent when you're still not even a dad may seem a bit of a stretch. But this activity taps into your deepest desires around what kind of a father you'd like to be. My guess: you'd like to be a deeply engaged and active dad. And while you'd probably like to goof off and get a bit rough-and-tumble at times, I suspect you're also looking forward to those sacred, tender moments where you see the miracle your child is and your heart just about explodes with wonder and gratitude. And that's a great goal! I highly recommend this approach, and so does so much of the scientific evidence that shows children of involved dads do better in life.

So no real downside exists to being an involved dad — and your involvement starts right from the beginning, with taking a keen interest in your partner's pregnancy. That's what this book is all about — enjoy the journey!

Dispelling Common Myths about Fatherhood

In the past, fathers were often effectively cut off from getting involved in parenting through preconceived ideas, peer pressure, or the demands of the modern workplace. Towards the end of the 20th century, however, we experienced a revival of fatherhood and the dawn of a new generation of dads — a generation of dads who were no longer content just bringing home the bacon and playing a supporting role in the rearing of their children.

Dads in the 21st century now have the option to do things differently and show the world they make fantastic caregivers. They want to be up to their elbows in parenting. Some dads are even taking over and sending mum back to the workforce. Something fundamental is changing about how we bring up our children and organise our lives.

However, despite the generation of new dads, many dads are still faced with a few persistent stereotypes that are taking way too long to die a slow death.

These include some of the following:

>> **Fathers are completely useless when it comes to looking after babies and children.** I want to say that this suggestion is garbage. But at the start, it's probably true for many of us men. Rarely have we grown up helping our parents raise our little siblings. And teen boys and blokes in their 20s don't tend to pick up the cute baby at family gatherings, sporting events, church, or down at the pub on Saturday arvo. So our experience and skills are often limited at first. But practice — time on the field — is how we get better.

Research shows that fathers are just as good as mothers at caring for babies once they've had a bit of practice and training. They're great with responding to their baby's needs and temperaments, and learning how to read baby's cues. And getting involved is worth it. Research also shows that children with involved dads do better in school, and are more confident and independent later in life. Yes, dads may parent differently from mums, but male ways of doing things are just as valid and important.

>> **Fathers don't have to do any of the day-to-day care that babies and children require.** This may be true if you want to remain in the dark ages of fatherhood. Twenty-first century dads do care-giving for one important reason: the best way to bond with your newborn child is by taking part in all that day-to-day stuff. Changing a nappy, trimming nails and bathing baby aren't just jobs that need to be completed; they're an ideal way for your baby to spend time with you and get to know you — and for you to get to know your baby. Your child learns that in times of need, you're there to offer safety, help her feel better, and comfort her when she's unwell or just needs a cuddle. Your baby learns words from you as you chat to her while she's in the bath, learns how to put clothes on from the way you dress her each morning and adopts all sorts of other good qualities simply from the way you are.

What builds your relationship with your baby aren't the big things, but the countless minor moments you have together. Consistency in the seemingly insignificant but important stuff is what makes you a great dad. Every single one of those 'insignificant' interactions counts.

>> **Mums think dads are incompetent.** This one may be true from time to time. But most mums really want to see dads step up and get involved. And, at the risk of falling back onto stereotypes, women may admire you just a little when you walk into that playgroup with bub on your shoulder. If you get the occasional overly 'helpful' mum in the supermarket who doesn't think you quite know how to handle a crying baby, be confident that you can demonstrate who's daddy by settling your little one with calm and competent compassion. Don't worry — I get to how you do that later.

>> **Fathers don't have a social life.** Wrong — fathers (and all parents) have a different social life. You may have to invest a

bit of time and thought into how you manage going out or taking part in sport or your other hobbies once you're a dad. Having an extra person in your life takes a bit of getting used to, but that doesn't mean you'll never be able to go out again. Working with your partner as a team and exercising a little creativity — while remaining mindful that your partner likely also wants to have a social life and needs your support to do it — is usually all it takes.

>> **Dads don't have a sex life.** Actually that one is kind of true, but only temporarily. The birthing experience, sheer exhaustion, and practicalities of looking after a newborn can make getting back to your pre-baby sex life with your partner somewhat tricky. And, for the safety of your partner, waiting a while to let her recover from the birth is important. The word here is patience. Rest assured: your sex life does return (check out Chapter 8 for more on this subject), and it will get better and better, even after kids. But you might just have to be a bit more creative now that your little one is in the house.

Knowing What Really to Expect

Asking someone to tell you what being a father is like is a bit like asking 'What does salt taste like?' Simply answering 'salty' may be true, but is unhelpful to anyone who hasn't tasted salt. How do you explain what being a father is like? The only answer is that it's like nothing you can explain — except, just like anyone who has tasted salt knows the taste, anyone who has been a father knows the feeling.

TIP

A good way to get an idea of what fatherhood is like is to spend some time with friends who have recently had a baby. And here's a novel idea for a lot of us men: talk to your parents and in-laws about it. They've been there. Their experience won't be the same as yours, but this can be an incredible opportunity to grow your relationship with them.

Similar to the uniqueness of your child's DNA, every father's experience is different. However, in the following sections, I run through some of the common factors of being a dad, the pros and cons you're likely to face, and some of the lifestyle changes you may have to make.

Understanding the dad experience

Here are some common factors that most fathers face:

>> **At first, you may feel like nothing has changed at all.**
Many new dads feel like this — and that doesn't make them
psychopaths who don't care. In fact, they can sometimes be
really troubled by the fact that they've just held their new
baby and now they're thinking about that 'thing' at work that
needs attention. Bonding, adjusting and really experiencing
the change that fatherhood brings takes time. Truth be told,
in the first hours and days after birth, many dads feel
overwhelming love for their partner but very little for their
baby. It takes time for the relationship to develop. But once it
does — at it could be a few months — you're never the
same.

>> **You often feel frightened, scared, overwhelmed and
sometimes lost.** Just changing a nappy for the first time or
getting clothes on a newborn feels awkward and wrong
when you're new at it. So what? Mums and all other dads
who get involved have the same experience. It really is just a
practice thing.

>> **Sleep becomes a big issue.** Babies don't understand that
day is for being awake and night is for being asleep. Over
time, your baby adjusts and eventually 'sleeps through the
night' — the Holy Grail for most parents. But a baby who
does this before six months of age is rare. Babies also need
nutrition every few hours to grow, so if your baby is waking
up in the night for feeds, consider that she's thriving and
growing is a good thing. Chapter 8 discusses feeding your
baby and getting her to sleep.

>> **You do things that you never thought you'd do.** You laugh
at things that seem completely ridiculous in hindsight, and
you might cry at times that you least expect. You also learn
lots about yourself and experience things that you can't
experience any other way. Fatherhood is truly an adventure.

>> **Sharing your partner's body with your child before and
after birth can feel a bit weird.** Sex during pregnancy can
be brilliant or a bit challenging, depending on your partner's
experience. And sex after birth can involve tackling some
new challenges. See Chapter 4 for more about sex during
pregnancy, and Chapter 8 for more on sex following birth.

LETTING GO OF BEST LAID PLANS

Parenting, for both fathers and mothers, requires a certain amount of letting go. When a baby is born, you no doubt want things for your child — the best of everything, and every opportunity and good thing in life that may come her way. You naturally want her to avoid the mistakes you made in your own life. But parenting doesn't work that way.

Many years ago, a taxi driver started chatting with me about parenting. When he found out that I write books for parents, he asked me, 'How do I make sure my son becomes a pilot?' I was intrigued. 'Does your son *want* to be a pilot?' I asked. He replied, 'I am not sure.' I paused as I considered where to take this conversation, and then questioned, 'How old is your son?' The response came: 'About 6 weeks.'

Making plans to try to set up your child for success is tempting. But more than anything, particularly in these early stages of your child's life, focus on the here and now. Be in the moment. Stay where your feet — and your child's feet — are. The nights may feel long as you battle sleep deprivation, but be assured, they fly by, and you will miss the laughter that makes your face crack no matter how hard you try to keep it straight, the cheeky smiles that light up your baby's eyes, and the joy that comes from being a dad to a newborn. More good things are coming. But what matters is soaking up what's right here, right now.

REMEMBER

Being a father is a lot about acceptance and going with the flow. A useful mantra to remember is 'This too *will* pass', because every illness, teething episode, period of sleep deprivation or colic will pass. In the moment, when you're weighed down with exhaustion, worry or fear, you might wonder whether it will or not. But it does. Looking after a baby teaches you a lot about life, and some fathers find that they're more relaxed, confident and happy as a result of having a child.

Considering the pros and cons of fatherhood

As with every life decision or change, good things and challenges exist. If you want to take a rational approach to fatherhood, consider the following.

On the plus side:

>> Fathers report their lives are more meaningful than before they had a child.

>> Fatherhood can make you a more compassionate, mature and confident person.

>> You get to be a child all over again. (Yes, you get to goof off, roll around on the floor, wrestle, play with cool toys and teach your child lots of silly tricks.)

>> You can hand down skills and values from your family. This is likely to feel deeply meaningful when you're nearing your final days.

>> You may for the first time in your life truly understand your own father.

>> You get a real kick out of raising a child well and seeing her achieve lots of things.

The challenges:

>> Until around three months of age, newborn babies are full on. They cry, sometimes for no apparent reason at all, and you feel like the sound is piercing your brain. Chapter 8 provides helpful hints about settling a newborn and coping with crying.

>> Sleep deprivation is common for all new parents. Fathers of babies under a year old typically have 42 minutes less sleep each night than other men. Doesn't sound like much, but it adds up. For ways to deal with sleep deprivation, again see Chapter 8.

>> You have less time for yourself and making plans really does mean making plans — spontaneity goes out the window a bit at the beginning.

REMEMBER

The upsides of fatherhood far outweigh the downsides, especially because most of the really annoying aspects (such as sleep deprivation) get much easier the older your children get.

A sad reality for a small percentage of Australian fathers is that they may not get the chance to experience all the joys that fatherhood has to offer. Though we don't often talk about miscarriage, stillbirth, premature birth and death in infancy in our society, these are terrible losses for some fathers to bear. Others have to deal with the fact that their child, so full of promise and hope, has a serious illness or disability that forces them to shift expectations of what being a father is all about and what their future brings. This grief can be overcome, and life can still be wonderful — and profoundly meaningful. I talk more about these issues in Chapter 9, and provide lots of information and support for parents.

Trading in your lifestyle (but not the sports gear)

Well, actually, I hate to say it, but you *may* have to trade in the sports gear too. Or at least use it a little less. Becoming a father is about changing your state of mind and changing your ideas of what's important to you. If you want a baby but don't want to change the way you live your life, you're probably better off waiting for a while to have children (keeping in mind that biology will have something to say if you wait too long).

Once you become a dad, some things inevitably change:

>> **Your work:** If you want to spend time with your family, you may consider working fewer hours, or changing to a flexible working arrangement that you can negotiate with your employer. Most dads don't make big changes, although a trend is forming around this. See Chapter 8 for more about finding a work–life balance.

>> **Your freedom:** Doing things when and where you want doesn't work when you've got a baby. If the swell is perfect and you just feel like going out for a surf, you may have to wait until your baby is asleep, or take her and mum along with you. Cycling with the bunch becomes trickier. And if you and your partner love the outdoors, that camping trip with the hiking or mountain biking might have to be postponed a year or two. Spending time out and about with your partner changes. Going out to dinner and a movie is no longer a spontaneous activity, but one requiring planning. Finding time for yourself alongside work and family commitments is one of the biggest challenges fathers face. Chapter 8 provides ideas for juggling other priorities after your baby arrives.

» **Your finances:** If you and your partner both had an income before your child came along, you're likely to be down to one income for a while. If you lived in a one-bedroom flat, you likely need to find somewhere bigger, and a way to pay for it. Some careful conversations might be necessary as you determine how to enjoy your new life with a baby without breaking the bank.

» **Your friends and family:** Your relationships with friends and family change. If you live away from your parents, you're likely to find yourself having to spend a lot more time travelling to visit them so your baby can see her grandparents (and you get a few hours of free babysitting). Your partner may have a deeper desire to be close to her mum. Some of your childless friends really embrace you having a child and become the fun aunt or uncle your child gets excited about seeing. Others aren't so keen and you see them less as a result.

» **Your holidays:** Going on holiday takes on a whole new meaning. You definitely have to postpone that backpacking trip around South America for a few years, at least until your kids are big enough to trudge alongside you. Family holidays are different — great fun, but unlike any holiday you've had since you were a child. And, ironically, they tend to be a lot of work – which makes them feel less like a holiday.

» **Your lifestyle:** Risky lifestyle or sporting activities such as big wave surfing, remote cycling, base jumping and free climbing are no longer just about risking your own life. You now have to consider the future of your child and family.

» **Your health and behaviour:** A child is one of the ultimate reasons to change unhealthy habits such as smoking, heavy drinking, eating junk food and being a slob. Children need a smoke-free environment to breathe in, good healthy food, clean clothes and nappies, and good hygiene to prevent illness. And watch your words too. Coarse language from a toddler might be funny the first time, but can be pretty awkward if it happens repeatedly. With babies and kids the process is pretty much 'monkey see, monkey do' — eventually all your behaviour comes back to you through your children.

Only Fools Rush In

Sometimes you can plan when you have a child, and sometimes nature has her own ideas. Either way, fatherhood is a big deal — fatherhood's not like buying a new pair of shoes or getting a plant. Your child, if you decide to have one, has only one shot at life and she deserves the best start you can give her. A positive, healthy, involved and reliable father is a big part of that. If you're being pushed into having a child by your partner or family members, talk it through with your partner. Don't just go along with it because you're afraid of the discussion. Becoming a dad is an important step in life, so take some time to figure out how you feel about it and share your thoughts with your partner.

How often in your life can you say you're really ready for something? Not often. Fatherhood, of all things, is probably the most difficult to feel truly ready for. Even if you've been planning to have a child, spent months going through IVF (see Chapter 2 for more about this) and been dreaming of the day you hold your child in your arms, the sledgehammer of reality is likely to whack you over the head when your partner goes into labour and you realise how not-ready you are.

If your partner is already pregnant but you don't feel ready for fatherhood, you've got time on your side. In the coming months, as your baby grows and gets ready for birth, read up on what's happening and what your partner's going through. (Chapters 3 to 5 run you through all the changes occurring for mum and bub in each trimester of pregnancy.) Find out more about the reality of labour, the interventions that might be required and what happens in the first few hours after birth. (Chapter 7 provides some great help here.)

TIP

During the pregnancy, spend some time with other people's children, talk to other fathers and let yourself ease into the idea of fatherhood. These are some of the most helpful things you can do to be prepared. Think about the kind of father your dad is and what you've learned from him. Think of all the things you would do differently.

If you're really, truly not ready for fatherhood as the birth approaches, talking to someone about your fears may help. Your midwife or GP can put you in touch with a counsellor.

CHECK THE NET

You can find a counsellor yourself through these organisations:

>> Family Relationship Services Australia www.frsa.org.au

>> Relationships Australia www.relationships.org.au

TIP

Don't forget to talk to your partner about what you're feeling. After all, you're in this together, so sharing your feelings and thoughts with her helps.

Sometimes, despite thinking that you'll wait to have a family until after a big project is completed, you've found a bigger house or you've been on that trekking trip to Nepal, nature jumps the gun. Your partner brings home a pregnancy test and you both find out she's likely pregnant. (Remembering home pregnancy tests need to be confirmed.) Crikey — you're going to be a dad. The key is to not panic. Freak out maybe, but don't panic (mostly because it takes a while for the baby to arrive). Okay, so you haven't painted the roof or skydived yet. Well, you never wanted to be one of those 'boring older people' anyway, so plenty of opportunities still exist to do whatever you want to do when your children are a bit older. Fatherhood doesn't mean you suddenly have to stay home every night whittling on the front porch — it just means your pace of life ticks along to a different clock.

Introducing the New-Generation Dad

Fathers today are a quantum leap from the previous generation of fathers. Twenty-first century dads push prams, get up for night feeds, change nappies, and have tried and tested burping techniques. We do everything — except for being pregnant, giving birth and breastfeeding. As for the rest of it, we can tackle anything. Dare I say it, dads can even do some things better than mums.

Dadhood: A good time to man up

All your life you've had just one person to take care of — yourself. You've made choices, taken risks and shouldered the consequences. But becoming a father is 'the big stuff'. You have a vulnerable, dependent, helpless child on your hands who needs you for the most basic aspects of her survival, such as food, warmth and love. And if everything's gone well, you also have a partner who needs you in a way you've never been needed before. To raise the stakes just a little further, your baby is also watching how you treat your partner — their mum — and the way you do sets the stage for what your child will expect from their partner. A lot is riding on how you do this stuff. Now's the time to stand tall, let go of your stuff, and be there for them — your family. (Does that sound weird? It's actually *your family!*) A real man makes the people around him feel stronger and safer. Fatherhood gives you the opportunity to do this in a way nothing else ever can or will.

Becoming a dad can add a profound sense of meaning to your life. Your views on life, priorities in the world and aspirations for your own future are forever altered. This is a good thing. By becoming a dad, you become part of the circle of life that has been going for eons. You're passing on the baton to your child, packed with all your wisdom and skills, to send your little one off on her own journey. You've got so much you can share with your offspring.

Children need dads. A Canadian study showed that having a father in a child's life helps her develop empathy. Another long-term study showed that a father's involvement with his child from birth to adolescence helps build emotional stability, curiosity and self-esteem. If you're going to have a child, be involved, committed and passionate about your new role. Your child deserves nothing less. She will feel stronger and safer if you're in her life in a positive, involved way.

Our children need involved fathers in their lives and, frankly, you owe it to yourself too. If you're going to be a dad, be a 100 per cent dad and experience it all. You wouldn't do other things in your life half-hearted, so get with it and give parenting your best shot. Make an effort, skill up and spend as much time as possible with your child. Doing so with all your heart makes you a better man.

Being a 100 per cent dad makes you a better man because it will stretch you and challenge you in ways you can't imagine. That's how we grow — through challenge, trial and adversity. But as daunting as that sounds, it's worth it. After all, who doesn't want to make more of themselves than they are now? Being a dad will do that for you.

Exploring care routine strategies

The question of how best to raise a baby is one of the most hotly contested subjects today. The rows of parenting psychology books on bookshop shelves attest to that. We've become disengaged over the last few centuries from listening to our instincts. We've let medical science overrule our hearts and minds, and slavishly followed rigid routines and overbearing doctor's orders that demanded that mother's convenience came first and baby's needs came second. We've joined the rat race and let work dictate our daily and weekly schedules.

If you think all the available information is a bit too much, you're probably right. Don't feel overwhelmed by the vast amount of 'expert' advice that everyone is trying to give you about how to raise your child. Reading up on stuff is useful, but at the end of the day you and your partner are in charge of your child — and decide how you want to bring her up.

Here are some common care routine strategies you may have heard of as you contemplate fatherhood:

>> **Strict routine.** In our mums' day, a strict routine with feeding and sleeping by the clock was promoted as being the best way to bring up a baby. Today, advocates of this method claim that having a strict routine or schedule establishes good habits early so you can detour sleepless nights and excessive crying. For some parents, routines work a treat and their baby easily slips into line. For others, their baby resists and parents end up even more stressed out that their little one won't play by the book. A strict routine is typically best for parents with twins or triplets.

>> **A routine, but not by the clock.** Babies need to feed and sleep at regular intervals but rather than let the clock determine when that might be, in this strategy reading your child's cues is the key to making the routine work. A pattern or routine of waking for a feed, feeding, having a nappy change, some play or awake time, and then back down for a sleep does occur. This pattern continues throughout the day, with no play or awake time at night. Chapter 8 has more about establishing a routine.

>> **Attachment parenting.** This form of parenting mimics parenting styles found in developing countries, where cots, bassinets and strollers are rare. Your child is in contact with you at all times of the day, is carried around in a sling or baby carrier, and sleeps with you at night, so she builds a strong bond and attachment with you.

REMEMBER

Many other strategies for raising a newborn exist. Do you leave her to cry when you put her down in order to teach her to fall asleep on her own, or rock her to sleep in your arms every nap time? Do you have the baby sleep in your bed, or have her in a bassinet in her own room? These are questions that you and your partner have to ponder and come up with your own answers to. And remember, there are the perfect 'text book' answers, and then there's the reality. You have to live with whichever strategy you come up with, so the strategy has to work for *you*. Chapter 8 gives you lots of ideas for raising a newborn.

TIP

Keep in mind that the way you want to run things in your family is up to you and your partner. Whether you adhere to a strict routine, or are a bit more laid back about it, as long as your little one is clean, fed and thriving, happy and cheerful, gets enough sleep, and is shown love and affection, she's going to be okay. Don't get caught in a trap of constantly comparing your baby to other babies; doing so generally leads to insecurity and stress and doesn't help you be a better dad. But ask questions of people who have been there, who have done it well, and who model great dadding. You need great guides. This book is one. They can be another.

Highlighting the Seven Attributes of Successful Dads

I've observed certain habits and attributes in amazing dads — and these are traits that each and every man can develop on his journey to becoming a father.

Here are my top seven habits and attributes:

>> **Willingness to have a go:** Feeling truly confident about handling a newborn takes time, but think about it. If you want to learn a musical instrument or a new language, you're

going to make a lot of mistakes. Maybe a million! Want to learn to be a great dad? Get your hands dirty (literally, in some cases), knowing you may get it wrong. That's how you learn. And it's also how you build that relationship. Don't feign incompetence and leave it to your partner. Have a crack. Show up. Get it done.

TIP

Can't get the nappy on properly? Have your partner, midwife or child health nurse show you. Then practice it ten times. You'll get it. If it's worth doing, it's worth doing badly until you can do it well.

>> **Selflessness:** After a life of doing the stuff you want to do, letting go of your agenda can be hard. The very best dads don't think less of themselves — but they do think of themselves less. While they are attentive to the needs of their little one, the most selfless thing they do is try to make life better for their partner. They find ways to serve and assist her, and lighten her load. They don't demand she think for the whole family. If you want to be an amazing dad, do stuff without being asked (such as cleaning the kitchen, making the bed, or running the bins to the bottom of the driveway). When she's overwhelmed, take the baby for a walk. This makes your relationship better and helps you be the best dad ever.

>> **Vision:** The best dads know who they want to be, and how they want to be. This matters, because when your baby is colicky, or wakes every few hours at night, or is teething and cries constantly, you may be at the end of your tether trying to work out how to put a stop to that noise. And without a vision of who and how you want to be, being less than your best is tempting. The truth is that often no solution is possible as you endure these challenges. You can't do anything to fix the problem or make a difference. It's just the way it is and you're going to have to suck it up. But understanding that everything in parenting comes and goes — that one day, your little one will sleep through, one day, your child will have all her teeth, and one day, she will grow out of colic — helps you endure the bad times while they last. And it's easier to do this well when you know who and how you want to be as a dad.

REMEMBER

The early weeks of a baby's life are a little like an endurance sport — just surviving the sleep deprivation, the crying that grips your brain and shakes it about, and the never-ending rounds of feeding, burping, changing and settling can seem impossible. But even marathons end sooner or later. The marathon runner has a vision for getting to the finish line and takes the steps to get there. It's the same with us as dads. You know you want to see that kiddo riding a bike, graduating school, finding a partner, and living a good life. You've just signed up for a two-decade marathon . . . so see the finish line and take the steps to get there.

>> **Perspective:** When your child is upset, it's easy to see things from your perspective. You're tired. You're stressed. Mum's falling apart. It's all too much. Why won't the baby just eat, sleep, poo, and leave you to live your life? Stepping back and seeing the world from your child's perspective — getting curious, not furious — will be your life saver.

TIP

Something happens when you pause and imagine life through your baby's eyes. Here's this kid . . . your kid. Non-verbal. Can't move. Needs something. Only one way to get it: scream. And while you're complaining, the gas in her tummy is building. Or the crap in her nappy has crawled up her back and it's burning her skin and stinking her out and feeling gross. Or she's got a pain but can't tell you where. And you're upset because you were halfway through watching a game of footy? Oh, and now she's getting your negative vibe and starting to feel insecure about herself. A shift in perspective where you imagine — with real empathy — what she must be feeling, is an attribute of the very best dads.

>> **Playfulness:** Immerse yourself in all the tasks that need doing around your baby, toddler and child and make it fun (so long as it doesn't upset bubba). Adding some playfulness means you're likely to develop a passion for being a dad. Your child picks up on your passion and is inspired to learn, develop and grow with you at an amazing pace. Play is one of the best ways for kids to develop and grow, and dads do playtime like a pro.

>> **Patience:** Patience is a virtue — especially for dads! Patience is your friend and makes things a lot easier when you've got kids around. Without patience, you can just pop with anger — cue tears all round, even for you. Most of the learning in the early years (and perhaps even throughout life) is achieved through constant and frequent repetition. As a father, you're in the business of facilitating that learning, which means repeating yourself a lot, such as reading *Where*

the Wild Things Are for the 53rd time, or telling your little one not to pour her milk in the fish tank for the 17th time. You can literally play peek-a-boo 400 times and your baby will still want more! As adults, we're often not great at dealing with constant repetition because it's deemed boring or frustrating, but repetition is just about the only way children can learn. By fostering your own patience you're able to elegantly deal with constant repetition and keep your calm. As a result, your child gets the support and encouragement she needs to learn. By being patient, you also avoid putting unnecessary pressure on your child to achieve something, which helps reduce frustration or feelings of inadequacy on her part.

>> **Presence:** Taking time to be with your child and partner as a family is important. How you spend that time with your family is also important. Children have a finely tuned awareness of your attention. They can tell right away if you're actually engaging with them or merely present physically, with your mind miles away. Being present means you devote 100 per cent of your attention to your child and you focus on what she's doing. You don't watch Netflix, scroll your Instagram reels or respond to emails at the same time as playing with your child. If you're hanging out with your child, be fully present and 'in the moment'.

To a child LOVE is spelled T-I-M-E. The best dads know this, and find a way to give it freely.

Chapter **2**

How to Make a Baby

Deciding to start a family with your partner is one of the biggest decisions you can make in your life (yes, bigger even than which footy team to support). For some, starting a family's not even a decision — it just happens. For others, just getting on the starting line of fatherhood is a journey, with the pregnancy and birth still to get through before you earn your dad wings.

Getting pregnant can be as easy as a few rolls in the hay or it can be a long struggle. But the important thing is that you and your partner approach the journey to parenthood together, even if talking about fallopian tubes and sperm counts isn't really your thing.

You probably think you know what's involved in conceiving a child, but my guess is that you're in for a few insights and surprises as you read this chapter. I start off with some useful sex tips, and then outline the journey your sperm makes before reaching his lady-in-waiting, the egg, and the mission that egg undertakes to get to its safe haven, the uterus. You find out tips and tricks to getting pregnant, and what options are available if things just aren't coming together. And, finally, once things are underway, I guide you through the process of getting sorted for the coming months.

Here Comes the Fun Part

You've probably worked out where babies come from by now. Making babies is fun — and so it should be! Not many projects in life start with a little nooky with your best girl. The rest of the journey may be exhausting, challenging or even frustrating at times, but at least this one first step can be all about a good time.

So go on, have sex, and lots of it. Not many manuals tell you to do that, do they? In this section, I run through some tips for conceiving naturally, how to improve the odds, and what to do if conception doesn't seem to be happening. But first, let's talk about sex in the 21st century.

Getting consent — and getting sexy

Here I run through a few tips and aspects to remember about the sex side of things. And they matter. Take note.

Checking in and asking for consent

First up, consent is king. And consent is sexy. You may think that because you've been in a relationship for a while, consent for your intimate activities is simply given. Not true. Your partner (or you, for that matter) may not always be up for it. Tiredness, stress, a disagreement between you both, monthly menstrual cycles or any number of other reasons might mean she's not keen. Being in agreement at all stages of your sexy time is vital. But — and this is a big but — you don't have to grovel, beg or plead. If your partner sighs, gives in and says 'fine', that's a pretty low bar.

TIP

Don't simply ask your partner, 'Do you consent to having sex with me?' Even if she did, she probably doesn't after a question like that. Instead, work consent into your sex. Walk up behind her as she gets ready for bed, for example, and run your hand up her neck and into her hair, massage the back of her neck, and ask, 'Do you like that? Would you like more of it?' As things heat up, check in with the same kinds of questions. Ask 'Would you like me to touch you there?' as you tease. Ratchet up the anticipation by *not* going for a home run (that's penetration, in case you missed the analogy) straightaway.

As you progress, keep gently checking in all along the way. Unless she tells you something along the lines of 'stop asking because you're ruining the vibe', consent is key. And you can turn it into a powerful and flirtatious aphrodisiac all the way along your foreplay and sexual journey. (The kink and BDSM community is *huge* on consent — and whether you're into that or not, you've got to admit that consent doesn't slow them down or get in the way of great sex.)

REMEMBER

Your partner may have some places she just doesn't want to go. Again, because you've likely been in a relationship for a while, you may know each other's no-go areas. But perhaps you're still exploring. A wide variety of sexual experience is waiting to be had, whether that be introducing sex toys or considering anal sex. As always, consent is king. Your partner may or may not like the idea of trying those things out. But if she's not keen, pushing, poking, and prodding may get you what you want in the short term, but will undermine your best efforts to have a healthy relationship in the long term. Nothing's less sexy than a guy pleading for a sex act his partner doesn't want.

Understanding your partner's build-up

To be clear, this is not a sex manual. But if you are with the woman you love and you plan on conceiving a child, you do want it to be a great experience — for both of you. Understanding that women's bodies prime differently to men's bodies helps with this.

WARNING

Pornography has delivered heterosexual men a script that says women want lots of penetration — and that penetration is staggeringly satisfying, they're always ready for it, and it leads to amazing and orgasmic outcomes. That narrative isn't helpful for most couples, and can actually harm your sex life.

While many men can go from a complete sexual standstill to all done and dusted in no time, powerful, positive sex for a woman can take *at least* 45 minutes. And to be clear, that's not 45 minutes of penetrative intercourse. That's 45 minutes of touching, playing, kissing, and so on. Patient and slow building of sexual tension and desire coupled with consent and communication usually leads to her satisfaction. And that, almost universally, will lead to your satisfaction. Making your partner happy by slowing down the process and making it about her will ultimately make it better for you both. So drop the porn script (if you've absorbed it) and learn to tease, taste and test. This will elevate your game with the woman you love, big time.

REMEMBER

A small percentage of women, regardless of their and their partner's best efforts, simply don't climax. If you and your partner need help in this area, seek medical or therapeutic help so you can work together to ensure your intimate lives remain positive and strong in this type of situation.

Knowing your partner's body

Another challenge we men face is that we can have a poor understanding of our partner's anatomy. I talk about female anatomy a bit over the next few pages, and understanding this area of your partner's body can really help as you move through pregnancy and beyond.

Chances are you've never really investigated her 'down there' bits closely. Perhaps some of what you do know comes from pornography, which probably isn't giving you the most realistic understanding. To improve this understanding, take a look at Figure 2-1, which shows the female genitalia.

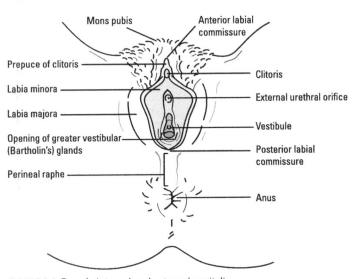

FIGURE 2-1: Female internal and external genitalia.

TIP

If your partner is open to it, you can even do some real-life explorations so you know the difference between her labia and her vagina, and you can determine the difference between her clitoris and her g-spot. Let her know you want to understand so you can help her enjoy your intimate moments more. Hopefully, you can have positive conversations that lead to understanding.

Conceiving naturally

Now let's get to the 'becoming a dad' part of sex. In an ideal world, just making the decision to 'start trying' would result in an instant pregnancy. But nature didn't make the process that easy. No sirree. Lots of barriers exist between your sperm and her egg; in fact, it's a miracle any of us were born at all.

Of the millions of sperm a man ejaculates during sex, only about 100,000 make it past his partner's cervix at the entrance to the uterus, having run the gauntlet of acidic vaginal secretions. (Figure 2-2 shows the female reproductive system.) Of the 100,000 sperm that get past the cervix, only 200 make it into one of the two *fallopian tubes* where a ready-to-be fertilised egg has made its way from an ovary and is waiting for a date — and that's *if* your timing is right and your partner is ovulating (producing an egg). Luckily, many sperm are present to start with because such a small percentage of them survive the journey. In the end, it's a merciless race to see which one of your sperm emerges as the champion and fertilises the egg by breaking into it.

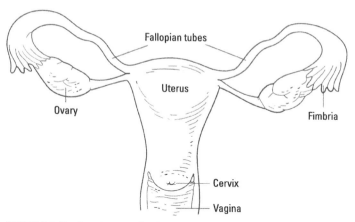

FIGURE 2-2: The female reproductive system.

Once the egg is fertilised, it moves down the fallopian tube and into the *uterus* or womb. Cell division starts and, before you know it (literally), the tiny cluster of cells begins nestling into the lining of the uterus wall, also known as the *endometrium* (see Figure 2-3). The cluster of cells then starts another long journey transforming into an *embryo*, and after eight weeks *gestation*, into a *foetus*. Bingo — your baby is on his way.

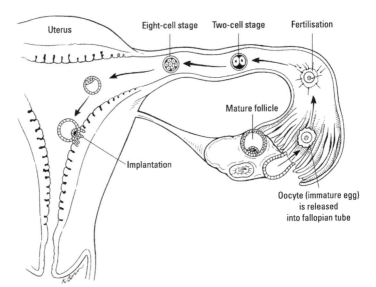

Uterus

Eight-cell stage

Two-cell stage

Fertilisation

Mature follicle

Implantation

Oocyte (immature egg)
is released
into fallopian tube

FIGURE 2-3: The journey of the fertilised egg from the fallopian tubes to implantation in the lining of the uterus wall.

Improving the odds — conception tips and tricks

Like a lot of things, getting pregnant is a matter of having quality equipment and good timing. Nail those and your chances of getting pregnant are pretty good.

But you can help things along with the following:

>> **Being fighting fit:** For prospective fathers as well as mothers, the healthier you are, the better for conception. Now's a good time to stop smoking, lay off the booze and other recreational drugs, get an exercise routine, and eat well. Doing those things can't hurt anyway.

>> **Staying put:** Try to ensure your partner doesn't get straight up for the 'loo routine' after sex! You partner can help those precious sperm get to their destination by keeping horizontal with her pelvis tilted upwards. While no scientific evidence shows that lying down after sex will increase the odds that you'll conceive, some evidence exists that standing up and heading to the bathroom can cause gravity to pull sperm away from their journey. The chances of it being an issue are

low, but it's good for your relationship to stay put for a short while anyway. So keep some tissues handy, cuddle up, and have some extra skin-to-skin time for about 15 minutes after it's all over.

» **Making a date:** *Ovulation* is when an egg is produced ready for fertilisation. The process occurs on approximately day 14 of a 28-day menstrual cycle, with day one being the first day of your partner's period. So plan for that time to be your 'sexy time'. If your partner's cycle is irregular or you just need more reassurance, try an ovulation test kit to tell you if the time is right for lurve. Ovulation test kits are urine tests that detect hormones, like a pregnancy test kit. Getting stuck into conversations around dates and timing can be kinda unsexy, so be intentional about flirting, sending sexy snaps, and upping the sexual tension so it doesn't turn into a 'just get it done' process. You want to enjoy this together, right?

» **Making sure your little fellows are in tiptop shape:** Have a health check. Your doctor can check for any signs of sexually transmitted disease, any anatomical problems such as an undescended testicle and any other issues you may not be aware of.

» **Checking on medication:** Prescribed medication as well as over-the-counter drugs can have a negative effect on mum or baby, so check with your doctor before taking anything during pregnancy.

» **Practising:** Have sex at least once a day when your partner is ovulating. If you feel a little put off by scheduled sexy time, just do it all the time — even in the off season. You never know what might happen. Being 'in the mood' for sex should also help conception! Finally, do some research on positions that aid conception and try them out — now that's an assignment you can enjoy!

Stress can affect your partner's ovulation, so try not to get too worked up about not getting pregnant straightaway. Good things take time and worrying about it won't make things happen any faster! Wanting to get pregnant is a great excuse for having lots of sex, so just enjoy it for a while.

REMEMBER

Health experts advise your partner takes *folic acid* if you're trying for a baby. Taking folic acid won't improve your chances of getting pregnant but it does improve your chances of conceiving a healthy baby. See Chapter 3 for more information about the effects of taking folic acid on your unborn baby.

Conception's not happening

You've been trying for months. And trying. And trying. But conception's just not happening. You're getting sick of sex — as if you ever thought that would be a problem. But, yep, you may be feeling exactly like sex is the last thing you'd like to do. As they say, too much of a good thing, and so on. So don't beat yourself up over feeling sex-tired.

WARNING

Couples under 35 years of age who have been having regular unprotected sex for a year and haven't become pregnant are said to be infertile, and those over 35 years old are deemed infertile after six months. If this is you, it could be time to talk to your doctor about getting some help. See the following section for more information about infertility.

Understanding What Can Go Wrong

Approximately one in six Australian couples has an issue with getting pregnant. A lot of factors in both partners can cause infertility, but here I just look at what factors could be affecting you. Around one in six guys across Australia experiences infertility, and problems on the male front can account for 40 per cent of 'infertile' couples not being able to get pregnant. Low sperm counts, blockages to the sperm being ejaculated, poor sperm motility, and sperm with an abnormal shape account for most fertility problems among guys.

Working out why conception hasn't happened

The following factors can contribute to infertility in men:

>> **Anatomical problems** such as erectile dysfunction or blockage caused by a varicose vein, called a *varicocele*, that connects to the testicle

- **Exposure to harmful substances** and heavy metals
- **Lifestyle**, such as smoking and drug taking
- **Overheating sperm** by having frequent hot baths or wearing tight fitting underwear or tight trousers (even jeans have been blamed for this)
- **Sexually transmitted diseases** such as gonorrhoea and chlamydia

REMEMBER

In 40 per cent of cases of male infertility, the cause may not be known. Either way, going for a check-up is a good thing to do. So be a man and own up to this task — if a problem exists, at least you know and chances are you can do something about it. This reduces stress overall and your partner definitely loves you even more for having a check-up.

REMEMBER

If the issue is not with you but your partner, try to be aware that this can be a rather rough time for her and she's probably feeling like a bit of a failure. A lot of women believe that being able to carry and nurture a child is an essential part of being a woman, and not being able to do this may leave her feeling inadequate. As her partner, you're in the best position to help her feel just as whole a woman no matter what.

Exploring other ways to get pregnant

If your partner is having trouble falling pregnant, the first step is to talk to your doctor. In some cases, lifestyle factors may be what are holding you back and if the problem is a blockage, surgery could help. But in other cases, you may need to consider *assisted reproductive technologies*, otherwise known as calling in the baby-making experts.

Some of the treatments you may want to talk about with your doctor or specialist include the following:

- **Artificial insemination (AI):** Semen is collected, given a bit of a clean-up, and then inserted into your partner's vagina, uterus or fallopian tubes. And, yes, you're the one responsible for delivering that semen sample into a plastic container — but, hey, it's all for a good cause!
- **In vitro fertilisation (IVF):** Your partner is given hormone treatments to kickstart her ovulation. When she is ovulating, your partner goes through a procedure where her eggs are harvested. The collected eggs are then mixed with your

sperm and given a chance to be fertilised. The fertilised eggs are put into your partner's uterus, and then you wait to see if they settle into the uterine wall.

>> **Intracytoplasmic sperm injection (ICSI):** Sounds sexy doesn't it? Rather than mix sperm and egg and wait to see which eggs are fertilised, sperm is injected straight into the egg. As with IVF, the fertilised eggs are placed into your partner's uterus, where hopefully one implants.

WARNING

If you use IVF or other assisted reproductive technology, be aware of the increased chance of multiple births. According to a recent report in the UK, on average one in four IVF treatments result in multiple pregnancies, compared with one in 80 naturally conceived pregnancies.

With IVF, sometimes two embryos are placed into the uterus, increasing the chances of having twins. In Australia, some clinics won't allow you to transfer more than two embryos. This is because the chance of complications during pregnancy and birth, such as premature birth or *pre-eclampsia* (a pregnancy complication characterised by high blood pressure), is higher with multiple pregnancies than with a single baby.

REMEMBER

About two-thirds of couples dealing with infertility do have a baby through these kinds of strategies, so medical intervention's definitely worth finding out about. Ask questions, even if doing so can feel a bit embarrassing at the start. By the way, this is good training for going through birth — many more embarrassing moments to come!

ADOPTING

You've been having sex on schedule for years now and had the tests to make sure your little guys are not only plentiful but frisky as well. Your partner has been through multiple cycles of IVF but it just hasn't worked out and all the trauma of not getting pregnant is way past its use-by date. Perhaps you've decided to give up on having a child of your own.

Being unable to conceive a child doesn't have to mean you can't be a father. Adoption is another option you can look at.

Adopting a child means you take on the parental rights and responsibilities of looking after that child as you would if you were his biological father. That's a lifetime's responsibility. Loving your own child unconditionally can be easy and you have to decide if you're able to do that for a child who's not biologically yours. Most adoptions these days are open adoptions, which means the child and his birth parents stay in touch with each other.

The number of babies who are put up for adoption in Australia is much lower than it was a generation ago — in fact, it's staggering low. In 2020–21, just 264 adoptions were finalised in Australia — including 42 inter-country adoptions and 222 Aussie child adoptions. Often the adoptions are of children already known to the family (through relatives). And adoption numbers have declined by around two-thirds in the past 25 years.

In Australia, each state has different departments that look after adoption services. Check the service in your area:

- **ACT:** www.communityservices.act.gov.au/ocyfs/children/adoptions/adopting-a-child-from-the-act

- **New South Wales:** www.facs.nsw.gov.au/families/adoption

- **Northern Territory:** nt.gov.au/community/child-protection-and-care/adoption

- **Queensland:** www.qld.gov.au/community/caring-child/adoption

- **South Australia:** www.childprotection.sa.gov.au/adoption

- **Tasmania:** www.communities.tas.gov.au/children/adoption/adoption_services

- **Victoria:** www.justice.vic.gov.au/your-rights/adoption/adopt-a-child

- **Western Australia:** www.wa.gov.au/organisation/department-of-communities/adoption-and-providing-permanent-care-child

Wow! You're Going to Be a Dad

Partner's boobs sore? Check. Period missed? Check. Thrown up for no reason? Check. That could mean you're going to be a dad (or your partner just had a really stressful week). Either way — don't panic. If your partner is really pregnant, you've got around nine months to sort out your new life. Say goodbye to how you currently live, farewell the days of tidy living rooms, sleeping-in, and endless hours of self-indulgence, and say hello to fatherhood! So with that in mind, a baby taking around 40 weeks to grow from a tiny cluster of cells into a living, breathing, crying baby is really a good thing. This time allows you to get a few things in order, indulge yourself or do some wild stuff before your baby arrives.

Getting confirmation

Your partner is likely to have raced off to the nearest pharmacy the moment she suspected she might be pregnant. Over-the-counter pregnancy tests can sometimes give inaccurate results, so even if you have a positive result from a test, the first thing you want to do is make sure the pregnancy thing is actually happening.

Make an appointment with your GP, who is likely to give your partner a urine test to see what levels of the hormone human chorionic gonadotropin (HCG) are present — that's the hormone thought to be responsible for the morning sickness and bone crunching tiredness your other half has to look forward to. If the test shows increased levels of HCG (that is, a positive result), your doctor may perform a gynaecological examination on your partner to check the physical signs of pregnancy more closely. But even your GP is only able to provide a definite answer when the pregnancy symptoms are clear, which is around four weeks after fertilisation. So holding off telling the world may be a good idea — in fact, you may want to wait until the first scan anyway. Find out more about ultrasound scans and breaking the news to others in Chapter 3.

REMEMBER

Once you've received confirmation of your pregnancy, a quiet (or loud) celebration with your partner is in order. However, it has to be a celebration unlike most you've likely had in the past because alcohol, cigarettes, and other drugs are definitely off the menu. But, hey — you can find plenty of other ways to have a good time. (Sex is definitely still *on* the menu!)

TIP

If you're both drinkers and you've decided that, for the health of the baby, your partner will stay off the drink, you might want to abstain in solidarity with her. The 'pregnant pause' campaign (pregnantpause.com.au) reminds mums and dads of the risks to baby when alcohol is mixed with pregnancy. The website also provides tips to help you be a great support to your partner by taking time off the grog so she doesn't feel like she's missing out.

Knowing what to do next

Welcome to the exciting new world of *antenatal*, or pre-birth, care. This was once strictly the domain of the pregnant woman and her doctor (usually male for some reason), but things have changed. For starters you as the dad are going to be much more involved (say 'yes!'). And you also have more choices about who you team up with for the journey to parenthood. Your GP can refer you to maternity services in your area and generally you have the choice of paying for care from a private obstetrician or midwife, or staying in the public health system with a hospital or independent midwife.

The role of your carer of choice is to guide you through the pregnancy, birth and early weeks of your baby's life. Your carer monitors the baby's growth and wellbeing, and checks for conditions such as pre-eclampsia and *gestational diabetes*. Your carer also works with you to come up with a birth plan (see Chapter 4 for more details on birth plans), delivers your beautiful new baby and helps you in the first few days after birth. This may include getting your partner started with breastfeeding or helping with basic baby care tasks such as bathing or changing a nappy. In general, your lead maternity carer is your 'go-to' person if you have any questions, health issues or just need someone to talk to during the pregnancy. So check with your carer first before contacting other services or professionals.

REMEMBER

Yes, a lot of attention during this time is on the mum-to-be. But that doesn't mean you can't ask questions and have a say in the kind of care your partner and unborn child receive. You, as dad, have a very important role in the making of your family, so don't feel embarrassed or afraid to ask about anything you're not sure of. The best thing you can do is be there, be helpful, and do some of the thinking so your partner doesn't have to carry the baby *and* the cognitive load of making the house and relationship function. Use your initiative — plan dinners, for example, organise outings or make the bed and do the laundry. Be helpful.

Things to do before morning sickness starts

Your life is about to change forever, so there's no time like the present to do some of those things you might have to trade in when your child is born.

To celebrate your impending fatherhood while you're not a father yet, think about the following:

>> Get in loads of unprotected sex (with your partner!).

>> Have the holiday of your lifetime. Holidaying won't be the same for the next 18 years or so (maybe longer, depending on how many kids you have), so make the most of your time now.

>> Ponder your own experience growing up and which things you would like your child to experience.

>> Sleep in late and cook a leisurely brunch for you and your partner regularly.

>> Splurge on something indulgent, such as going to a fancy restaurant or a day spa.

>> Start a blog or scrapbook to document the months leading up to your child's birth and make it a memento to give your child when he's older (yes — plenty of good material for an embarrassing 21st birthday slideshow).

>> Skill up on massage techniques and practise on your partner. Invest in a few good-quality aromatherapy oils and some sweet almond oil.

2

What to Expect When She's Expecting

Focus on your baby's development through each trimester of pregnancy.

Understand all the medical terms being thrown around and help your partner deal with common side effects during each stage — knowledge is power!

Find out all the pregnancy secrets worth knowing — including which baby gear is actually useful.

Chapter **3**

The First Trimester

Pregnancy is a bit like *The Lord of the Rings* trilogy: it has a beginning where the scene is set and a bit of chaos occurs, a middle where things calm down a bit and an end where everything comes to a head. The three distinct parts are called *trimesters* and each has its scary and great bits (just like in the films), such as the first time you hear your baby's heartbeat at a check-up, feel your baby kick inside mum's belly, or see your baby's squashed up body twisting and turning on an ultrasound screen.

The easiest part of becoming a dad is the pregnancy bit. Fortunately for us, we don't get the morning sickness and leg cramps, and we're not the ones who sometimes feel as if they can't get out of bed without a crane. By the end of the pregnancy, you're probably going to be right on top of what aches this week, or what bizarre food your partner has to have *right now*.

But that's not to say we can't do anything during pregnancy. Apart from all the preparations (which I talk about in Chapters 4, 5 and 6), you can do lots of stuff with your partner to help her out a bit and to get to know your offspring (yes — before she's even born!). Your partner definitely needs a strong man for the finale: 'birth' (which I cover in detail in Chapter 7).

In this chapter, I take you through the first trimester and tell you a bit about what your baby is up to on the inside. I also take the mystery out of morning sickness and explain why your partner may experience sore boobs.

Eating Enough to Make a Baby

During pregnancy, your partner is literally 'making the baby', so good ingredients are essential for a quality end product, meaning that your unborn baby needs good food. Mum's healthy diet during pregnancy has a profound impact on the wellbeing of your little one even later in life, so work on healthy food choices together.

Don't let any diet discussion turn into an awkward 'control' scenario. A bloke dictating his partner's food choices or creating guilt in her by food shaming is an ugly thing.

The best way to navigate this diet conundrum is to ask your partner how she wants to approach diet over the next 30 to 40 weeks, and go all in with her. For you, this may mean also laying off unhealthy options — because nothing is worse than tempting a pregnant woman with food and drink she can't or shouldn't have.

Mum also needs good food to help her deal with the physical, mental, and emotional changes and challenges she faces until your baby is born.

The 'eating for two' approach is another pregnancy myth — no matter what Great Aunt Beryl may tell you. The female body requires 10 to 12 per cent more energy when pregnant.

So, what is 'good food'? Your partner needs the following:

>> **Six servings of fruit and vegetables:** An apple or tomato is a serving, so is half a cup of salad. Leafy green vegetables are particularly good because they contain folic acid, which helps prevent birth defects such as spina bifida (see Chapter 9 for more about birth defects).

>> **Six servings of grains:** A cup of cooked pasta or rice, or a slice of wholegrain bread or a bread roll makes a serve. Wholegrains are particularly useful because — you guessed it — they contain folic acid. (In September 2009, Australia

introduced folic-acid enriched breadmaking flour. New Zealand followed suit in 2021.)

>> **Three servings of dairy:** A large glass of milk, a tub of yoghurt or two slices of cheese are each a serve.

>> **Two servings of protein:** An egg, or two slices of lean red meat, or two chicken drumsticks are one serving. Vegetarians can also get protein from nuts and seeds, legumes and tofu.

Folic acid, also called folate, is a B vitamin that's important to help prevent birth defects such as spina bifida. Eating folate-rich foods such as wholegrains, chickpeas, leafy green vegetables, and Vegemite helps you reach the recommended daily allowance of 500 micrograms (0.5 milligrams). Your partner can also top up her folic acid intake by using vitamin supplements. Check the recommended amount of folic acid for your partner because some women in a high-risk category need more.

Mums shouldn't eat certain foods because of the risk of bacteria, such as *Listeria monocytogenes*, to which pregnant women and unborn babies are extremely vulnerable. So don't go treating your partner to:

>> Any cooked food that's been in the fridge for more than 12 hours

>> Cold sliced meats (such as hams and salami) or pâté

>> Ready-made salads (fresh and homemade salads are a good alternative)

>> Soft cheeses such as brie, ricotta and blue vein

>> Sprouted seeds

>> Sushi

>> Unpasteurised milk

Ask your GP, obstetrician or midwife for a comprehensive list of foods to avoid.

By the end of her pregnancy, your partner may be really hanging out to eat a good bit of brie again, so a great way to celebrate the baby's birth may be to put together a platter of the things your partner's been missing out on for nine months. Start a 'foods to remember after birth' list.

Dealing with Common Side Effects in the First Trimester

For some unfortunate mums, the first three months of pregnancy are a downright drag and can feel like an illness rather than the beautiful natural process of creating life. No glow can be seen and no bump is present to show off. Instead, as your baby makes herself comfy in your partner's uterus, she's making her presence known in other ways. Symptoms vary wildly from woman to woman, so you have no way of exactly knowing what's going to hit your partner. The following sections cover some common complaints.

REMEMBER

Some women don't have any of these issues, and some have them at level 10! Your partner not having strong symptoms isn't a sign of problems. On the other hand, if your partner is struggling, think about how you want her to react to you when you have a serious case of 'man flu'. (We all know how serious that can be, and how much pampering we need when it strikes.) Your partner needs that same level of love and care to get through this. But while man flu only lasts a few days or a week at most, this pregnancy sickness can go the distance.

Jokes aside, care during pregnancy is really serious for you, your partner, and your baby. In the most significant cases, these issues can occasionally be life-threatening. Be involved, and listen to good quality, specialised medical advice on this stuff. If you have any concerns, involve your medical professionals.

REMEMBER

During the next nine months, you're going to learn a whole new vocabulary and get to know your partner's insides more than you may want to. The Glossary lists terms to help you decipher what your carer of choice is talking about. If you're unsure of where the various parts of the female reproductive system are located, refer to Chapter 2.

Morning sickness

Morning sickness typically involves feeling nauseous and vomiting. The condition is common and is usually experienced during the first three months of pregnancy. Morning sickness doesn't pose a risk to the baby unless it's very severe. Morning sickness is thought to be caused by those crazy pregnancy hormones and usually subsides after 12 weeks, though not always. (Painfully — for everyone — it can last the whole 40 weeks in some cases.)

Nausea can come on at any time but is usually worse in the morning because your partner's stomach is empty. At its worst, morning sickness is like having a hangover and being seasick at the same time, so no wonder your partner is off to the bathroom once again. If you're like me, you'd choose death or swimming back to dry land over being seasick, so try to get your head around how rough morning sickness must be! (Bathrooms also become a prominent feature in the last trimester, albeit for different reasons — your partner needs to wee what seems like every ten minutes because the baby puts pressure on her bladder.)

TIP

One thing that makes morning sickness worse is getting up on an empty stomach, so try having a plate of dry crackers or toast with Vegemite ready for your partner to nibble when she first wakes up. Other tips include eating smaller portions more often during the day, increasing intake of carbohydrates and reducing intake of fats, and stimulating pressure points on the inner arm just above the wrist crease.

WARNING

Morning sickness can get so bad that your partner may become dehydrated. The symptoms aren't always easy to spot so double-check with your midwife, obstetrician, or GP if your partner is having a really rough time with morning sickness. In particularly serious cases, medical carers may recommend hospitalisation. It can be that bad!

Exhaustion

Your baby is growing rapidly. Believe it or not, it takes a lot of your partner's energy to keep this process moving along. Just getting through a day at work may be more than your partner's up to, so you can score lots of points if you take on more of the household chores, prepare meals, and do the things your partner's not up to doing. Bonus points if you do it without being asked.

Heightened sense of smell

Pregnancy does strange things to a woman, not least of all her ability to smell everything. Your partner can walk into a room you left three hours ago and smell your aftershave. She's likely to be sensitive to most smells, especially things such as perfume, food and petrol fumes — they may even make her vomit —so if you're heating your favourite garlic bread (the one with extra garlic and blue cheese), open a window or put on the range hood.

Tender breasts

What was your favourite dessert when you were growing up? Do you remember seeing the dessert, in the fridge or cooling on the bench, hours before dinner, and being told you could 'look, but don't touch'. For many expectant dads, the same concept might now apply in the bedroom. Pregnancy hormones cause your partner's breasts to become a bit bigger, but in some cases they're sore and tender. So while you may be admiring your partner's new wonder boobs, it pays to wait until she invites you to party before gatecrashing her bra.

REMEMBER

Consent, as always, is king. And, in most cases, the tenderness and pain does subside — which means you'll both enjoy several months of booby bliss.

Moodiness

Blame any moodiness during pregnancy on the hormones. Your partner hasn't turned into a grumpy, unpredictable monster — she's just at the mercy of her body. Go easy on her if she's a little ratty right now. Talk to her and figure out a way to communicate when she's feeling emotional or grumpy, because *progesterone*, the hormone responsible for all this, isn't going to go away for a long time yet.

TIP

A gentle way forward is to name or describe how she's feeling (with empathy), and ask if she wants space or company. You might simply say, 'It's been a rough day hasn't it. You're feeling awful. Would you like me to stay and be close to you, or do you just need space?' Note that sometimes the moodiness will be so utterly challenging that she may not know what she wants. If that's the case, hug her until she asks you to leave. But remember that if she does tell you to leave, it's not about you. It's not personal, it's pregnancy. Stay low key. Don't pressure her to cheer up. Just be there until it passes.

ACTIVITIES TO AVOID

Some activities aren't recommended for mums-to-be, such as:

- Going on rides in theme parks (because of the acceleration the body experiences during the ride)

- Extreme sport and adventure sport (such as bungee jumping, parachuting and wild water rafting)

- Dyeing her hair (because of the chemicals used in dyes)

- Travelling on a plane (in case the baby decides to arrive early, although this is mostly relevant towards the end of the pregnancy)

For a comprehensive list of things to avoid, ask your GP, obstetrician or midwife.

REMEMBER

Though your partner's feeling crappy, this is your chance to shine. You can treat your partner and make her feel special in lots of simple ways at this difficult stage. Come home with a little gift (baby socks are great), shout her a pregnancy massage (along with some nice oils to battle stretch marks), or get a nice DVD for the night (avoid *Alien*). If your partner bites your head off for trying, don't take it personally. Try again next week.

Finding Out What Your Baby's Up To

Between 6 and 12 weeks, your baby grows from 6 millimetres long to 5.5 centimetres long (see Figure 3-1). In other words, your baby has grown 900 per cent in six weeks. No wonder your partner is so tired.

During this time, your baby's organs take shape, with the heart beating from about six weeks. Though neither you nor your partner can feel her yet, your little tadpole (babies look like that at the beginning) is moving around in there. She's floating in amniotic fluid in her amniotic sac. The placenta is developing to act as life support for your baby.

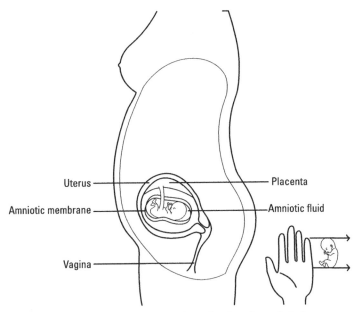

FIGURE 3-1: At 12 weeks, your baby is about the size of your little finger.

REMEMBER

Your first ultrasound scan, which typically happens between 6 and 12 weeks after conception, is a pretty big deal for a couple of reasons. First, you get to see your baby for the first time ever and it's an amazing sight. Second, in some cases, your doctor may unfortunately advise you that something isn't quite right. This happens in about one in six cases and may result in miscarriage or termination of the pregnancy for medical reasons (see the sidebar 'Dealing with the grief of miscarriage').

REMEMBER

Significant decisions need to be made in relation to termination or abortion, so seek medical advice (and any other advice from trusted confidants) and be sure you and your partner are on the same page.

Your doctor typically prepares you before your first scan, but talking about this scenario with your partner before you have your scan is a good idea.

DEALING WITH THE GRIEF OF MISCARRIAGE

A miscarriage is the death of a baby before 20 weeks gestation. Many women don't even know they're pregnant when they miscarry, but many others lose much-wanted and cherished babies. In the past, people have had the attitude that miscarriages are something to be gotten over, and that everything is fixed by trying for another baby. As men, we'll never understand just how deeply a miscarriage affects the baby's mother — our partner. The effects of miscarriage can be profound. While I would never engage in a comparison game, we do need to recognise that fathers can also be deeply impacted by the loss of a baby they'll never have the opportunity to hold and to raise. The grief that comes with the lost future of that child can be overwhelming. Having healthy ways to grieve is important for men as well as women. One thing to be aware of is that someone just getting 'over it' is rare. Give yourself and your partner the time necessary to grieve.

If you grapple with this devastating loss, you will also likely feel you have to be strong for your partner . . . and in a sense you do. You need to advocate for your partner at a time when she's confused, angry, vulnerable and grieving. But you also need to be empathetic and caring, and one way to do that is to talk openly about your feelings with your partner. You also need to acknowledge your feelings of loss and sadness, rather than pretend to keep a stiff upper lip. You may have heard the phrase, 'If it's mentionable, it's manageable'. If you can mention how painful things are, you can start to process them more effectively. Talking also offers what psychologists call 'psychological distance', and allows you the space you need to step back and see your pain for what it is, rather than living in it. Remember, though, that your focus may need to be on your partner and her grief for a time.

Having a ceremony or funeral for your lost baby may be comforting and give you a chance to express your grief and let others support you. The ceremony can be anything from a few people lighting a candle, to a funeral with a minister or religious leader. Just do what comes naturally to you and your partner. Naming your baby can also help you heal — acknowledging your baby as a real person, not a 'loss' or an 'it' can really help.

(continued)

(continued)

If you need to talk to someone outside your family and friends, support is available. You just have to ask for it.

In Australia, contact the following:

Bears of Hope: An organisation that offers grief wellness groups in your local area and grief counsellors, free of charge, for people who have lost a baby during pregnancy, birth or infancy. Visit www. bearsofhope.org.au or call 1300 114 673.

Sands: An independent organisation that provides support for miscarriage, stillbirth and newborn death. Go to www.sands.org. au or call them on 1300 072 637.

Getting the Right Gear

The first trimester is also a perfect time to familiarise yourself with the stuff a baby needs (you have to do it eventually so it's a good idea to get a head start on this task). The first thing you're likely to notice is that babies need an unbelievable amount of stuff. Unless you have unlimited funds available, finding out about what babies need and being somewhat rational about buying baby gear is very useful. I've done the heavy lifting for you and in the following sections you find out what you really need and what's pure luxury.

To start with, a great idea to keep costs down is to send the word around among your friends and co-workers that you're having a baby. They may have cots, bassinets, and strollers they're no longer using. You can completely kit out a nursery for very little or even for free. And places such as Facebook Marketplace or other online pages can be amazing for finding low-cost, high-quality, pre-loved gear. You might want some things to be new, but most items don't need to be, and your baby quickly grows out of others, so save where you can.

Clothes and shoes

Baby clothes come in more shapes and styles than you would have thought possible. Check out what works for you before you spend up large. As well as the usual T-shirts, singlets, jumpers and trousers that children and adults wear, babies have these kinds of clothes to keep them decent:

» **Bodysuits** are long- or short-sleeved T-shirts that do up around the baby's crotch with domes (clips or press-studs). They're handy for keeping everything tucked in so bub's tummy doesn't get chilly if a top starts riding up. They're also great during the summer months when a short sleeved bodysuit can be worn by itself without pants or as pyjamas. The only drawback with bodysuits is that if your baby is fully dressed and has a nappy leak, you have to take everything off to change her, rather than just her pants. And this stuff can get messy. But the pros outweigh the cons here.

» **Stretch-n-grows** are all-in-one trousers and tops that either dome up the legs and front, or zip up. They're like an overall with socks. Some dome up the back, which is really inconvenient — steer clear of them. Most have feet, but you can get stretch-n-grows without feet for summer.

» **Sleeping bags** are like stretch-n-grows with sleeves but no legs, just a sack covering your baby's legs and feet. They're handy in winter when your child is able to roll over and kick around in bed. Your child inevitably kicks off her wrap or blanket so having her wear a sleeping bag means she doesn't get as cold. Sleeping bags are also good because if her legs are bare under the sack, you can get to her nappy more easily and disturb her less at night.

The following list is a guide to what you should have ready to go for your newborn baby. You can customise your list as you find your dad–legs and suss out which items work well for you. You can also tweak the list to suit the seasons. As a general rule, baby clothes should be loose–fitting, made with breathable and soft fabric, and easy to open and close. Remember you can go through three to four sets of clothes in a day because of nappy leaks and baby spew.

Here are the items you need:

» Lots of singlets, either cotton or woolly for cold winters.

» Four bodysuits, both long- and short-sleeved, or long- or short-sleeved tops if bodysuits don't appeal.

- » Four pairs of trousers. Overalls are pretty cute but make sure they have openings in the legs so you don't have to take the whole lot off to change her nappy.

- » Four stretch-n-grows or sleeping bags for night time. Check that they are cotton, rather than polar fleece or microfleece, because those fabrics aren't breathable and she may get overheated.

- » Two jackets for going out.

- » Two cardigans or wraparound jerseys that don't need to go over her head.

- » Lots of pairs of socks — typically one sock of a pair always gets lost.

- » Four hats, preferably made of a lycra-cotton mix so they stretch, or lovely soft wool if they're handmade.

- » Lots of bibs with either domes or Velcro. Bibs with ties can prove too fiddly.

- » Two pairs of slippers that have elastic around the heel. These stay on better than other slip-ons. Babies don't need shoes until they're walking.

- » Two pairs of gloves or mittens. Get some that you can tie around the wrist because babies tend to lose them (intentionally and unintentionally).

Here are some valuable tips for selecting clothes and making dress-up time easy (on you and the baby):

- » Most babies get grumpy at having clothes pulled over their heads. Avoid anything that doesn't have a few domes opening at the shoulder or an envelope-style neckband (two overlapping pieces of fabric that stretch easily when put over her head) to make pulling the clothing over her face painless.

- » When putting on a stretch-n-grow, cardigan or any other top that doesn't go over your baby's head, lay the item on the surface you're dressing your baby on before you lay her down. Then all you have to do is slide her arms into the sleeves, dome her up and you're good to go.

- » Avoid anything that has a back opening. Your baby spends a lot of time lying on her back in the early months and having domes under you can't be comfortable. They're also tricky to get on when you're getting her dressed.

- Avoid anything that looks too fiddly. Some babies really dislike getting dressed and trying to do up silly little ribbons when she's having a meltdown isn't a good time for anyone.

- If your baby arrives in winter, look for clothes that have folds sewn into the ends of sleeves — they're actually mittens. As well as helping keep her warm, these are great to keep your bub from scratching herself with those blade-like newborn nails.

- If in doubt on sizing, buy clothes that are too big. At least you know junior is going to grow into them. (See the sidebar 'How many 0s can you go?' for information about size labels on baby clothing.)

- If you've been given a lot of hand-me-downs, be aware that the fire retardant in some clothing may be worn and not be as effective as it is in new clothes.

- You're likely to be given a tonne of new clothing as presents, so if you find you have too much, don't be afraid to take it back to the shop and swap it for something you can use in the future, like the next size up.

- Dark colours show baby spew much more than light colours, but light colours show baby poo much more! Just go with what colours you like.

REMEMBER

Handling a baby during the first few months can feel a bit tricky because she can appear really fragile. So think about what steps you need to go through to put on a particular item of clothing. If the clothes seem complicated to close or open, don't buy them. Don't be afraid to try out the garment in the shop with a baby doll.

TIP

If your baby is premature, look for more 0s when you're buying clothes. Clothes are often labelled '00000' or the label says 'premature'.

Your baby won't need shoes for a while yet. A good time to start looking for shoes is when your little champ starts crawling. Studies show that going barefoot is best — but that's not always practical. For a baby who isn't walking yet, soft-soled shoes with an elasticised heel work well and protect toes from being scraped on the floor or ground. But as she starts walking, her footwear needs to change gradually towards firmer shoes.

HOW MANY 0S CAN YOU GO?

If we lived in a perfect, logical world, clothing labels for babies would give an age range to show the size of the item. But because all babies are different, labels show 0s instead.

Until she's one, your little one is going to be less than zero, or many zeros. Here's how it usually works:

- **0000:** Birth to three months, or newborns under four kilograms
- **000:** Three to six months, or babies four to six kilograms
- **00:** Six to nine months, or babies between six and eight kilograms
- **0:** 9 to 12 months, or babies from eight to ten kilograms
- **1:** 12 months, or babies over ten kilograms

Here are some tips and tricks for buying your baby's first pair of shoes:

>> Choose shoes with one centimetre of wiggle room at the front and end, but no more than that — she'll trip over her own feet.

>> Look for shoes that are as similar to bare feet conditions as possible. She doesn't need arch support at the beginning!

>> Babies' feet get hotter and sweat more than adults' feet, so choose natural breathable materials rather than synthetics.

>> Soles that grip are important too, as junior needs all the help she can get to not slip when she's learning to walk.

Strollers, prams and buggies

Prams have evolved into high-tech, fold-at-the-touch-of-a-button contraptions that can double as shopping trolleys, have water bottle holders, be taken off-road, and cook you lunch (just kidding on that last part). Baby stores are packed with different models of prams and strollers. A pram and/or stroller is often one of the bigger purchases you make in this fatherhood game, so shop around.

Some research suggests that babies in prams that face towards you rather than out into the world are better — at least for the first nine months or so — because your baby is less stressed. Facing each other also encourages more talking, laughing and social interaction. Many from-birth prams have both rear-facing and forward-facing positions.

Some of the things you need to look out for include the following:

>> Can you dismantle the pram and put a car seat or bassinet attachment on it in the early months, making transferring junior from bed or car seat easier?

>> Does the stroller come with a fitted sunshade and fitted weather cover?

>> Does the stroller fit through the door of your favourite cafe? Can it be easily manoeuvred through a packed supermarket? If you're looking at three-wheeled prams, make sure the front wheel isn't fixed so you can manoeuvre the pram easily.

>> How easy is adjusting the back of the seat? Can bub lie down flat in the pram for sleeping? Can the back be raised up high for a growing child to see more of the world around them?

>> How easily can the pram fit in your car boot or in your house? Some models can be bulky.

>> How easily does the pram fold down? The last thing you want is to be pulling levers all over the place when you've got a fussy baby to deal with. If you're travelling by public transport, strollers that can be folded down with only one hand are ideal so you don't have to hand your baby to a total stranger while you wrestle with getting the stroller on board.

>> How well does the pram support your child's growing spine and neck?

>> How well can the pram survive if you want to take it on unpaved walkways or bush walks?

KNOWING YOUR BUGGY FROM YOUR PRAM

Confused about what's a pram, what's a buggy and what's a stroller? Then read on!

In Australia, most people refer to baby carriages as prams; in New Zealand and the US, most people call them buggies or strollers. Some people say a pram is used for a baby carrier that only allows your baby to lie flat, while a stroller is used for anything that allows her to sit up. Whatever you call them, they're substantial beasts, sometimes with three wheels, sometimes four. Prams and strollers are quite cosy and comfortable for your child, and have an adjustable back so that your tyke can lie down or sit up. Many models allow baby to face out to the world and face you (with the position being adjusted depending on the baby's age). Many models also have a carry cot–type set-up, so you can instead sling a bassinet on the frame when your baby's still wee.

A compact stroller is not so heavy and can be folded width-ways quite easily. These strollers don't have a push bar at the back, but two handles like the handle of an umbrella, which are really handy if you travel by public transport and have to fold the stroller when you get on, or if you're a frequent flyer. Some people even refer to them as 'umbrella strollers'.

Whatever mode of transport you choose for your baby, make sure that it meets Australian/New Zealand standard AS/NZS 2088:2000. Prams and strollers are designed to move freely, so always ensure that you're holding onto the pram or that the brakes are on when you've stopped moving. In Australia, prams and strollers are now fitted with a tether strap to help you keep control over the pram (you can also buy tether straps where you buy prams). The Australian Competition and Consumer Commission pamphlet 'Prams and strollers — safety requirements' provides helpful information on pram/stroller safety and is available on its website (www.accc.gov.au).

Car seats

Getting a cute mobile for your baby's cot is optional, buying a stroller that you can take mountain running is optional — but using a car seat for your most precious cargo is not. Yeah sure, you may have free ranged in your parents' car when you were little and lived to tell the tale, but sadly some children haven't. So take advantage of the fact things have evolved somewhat since 'the good old days' and use a car seat for every journey you take in the car with your baby. Besides, it's the law.

Different sizes of car seat for the age and weight of your child are available, generally falling into these categories:

>> **Baby capsule:** This is a car seat shaped like a cradle that is used for newborns up to six months or weighing eight kilograms. The capsule is strapped into the car using the car's existing seatbelts and is rear-facing.

A baby capsule can be taken out with your baby in it and attached to the top of special shopping trolleys and some strollers. Baby capsules also have a movable handle so you can carry your bub around in it like Red Riding Hood's basket of goodies.

>> **Child car seat:** From 6 to 12 months (weight 8 to 12 kilograms), babies should still be in rear-facing car seats. Many rear-facing models can be converted to front- facing after bub's first birthday or once they weigh in the 9 to 12 kilogram range. Car seats usually have a strap that attaches to a bolt in the back of the back passenger seat. If your car doesn't have a bolt, they can be purchased and put into the car by a mechanic for very little money.

From 12 months to four years children must use a rear-facing or forward-facing child car seat with an inbuilt harness. Smaller kids are often best to remain facing the rear for a longer period of time.

>> **Booster seat:** When your child reaches 18 kilograms or her shoulders are too wide for her car seat, she can move to a booster seat. Children are required to be in a booster seat with an adult lap-sash seatbelt or child safety harness.

REMEMBER

Using your child's size as a guide, rather than just their age is always best when considering car and booster seats. Don't move small kids up to the next level just because they're older. Safety matters here.

CHECK THE NET

As an alternative to buying a car seat, check out Hire for Baby (www.hireforbaby.com).

As with strollers, so many models of car seats are available that shopping around pays. Luckily you've got a few months to do this!

If you're buying a second-hand seat, check the safety regulations with the road safety authority in your state or territory to make sure the seat is up to scratch.

Toys

When your baby is born, all she does for a while is poo, pee, eat, cry, sleep and gaze benignly at things. So she doesn't need an electronic ABC, a racing car set or a mini piano — and she definitely doesn't need an iPad. What she needs are things that give her a real sense of the world she's just come into — new sights, shapes, textures, smells, sounds and sensations. These can easily be provided by spending time with your baby, singing to her, and touching her skin and fingers with textures like an old comb, fabric, your hair, leaves, the cat's fur — you get the idea. As she begins to grasp and bring her hands together, things like a rattle or a chain of plastic rings can keep her fascinated for ages.

When your baby starts teething, she looks for things to put in her mouth to push against her gums to relieve the discomfort. Many toys double as teething rings and aids.

Some good ideas for baby toys include

>> **Balls and blocks:** Great for giving your newborn an idea of basic shapes.

>> **Cloth books:** Look for ones with flaps or textures sewn into them.

>> **Plastic keys:** For some reason, babies love your car keys, so give your baby her own set. These are great for teething, too.

>> **Play gyms:** Play gyms are mats with arms curved over the top where you can attach colourful objects such as paper flowers, branches from the garden, soft toys and strings with large shells for your baby to look at as she lies on the mat. Just make sure she can't pull anything down that she shouldn't be chewing on. Nothing is safe from her gummy mouth once she's got the hang of her hands.

>> **Rattles:** You can buy rattles or make your own from old plastic containers filled with rice. Ensure the lid is on securely.

>> **Soft toy animals:** Avoid fluffy toys with long hair or fur.

REMEMBER

Less is more when it comes to toys — no matter what the toy manufacturers tell you, nothing beats spending time playing and exploring with your baby. Your baby's brain development is assisted by appropriate stimulation and human contact . . . not by any particular gadget.

WARNING

To make sure toys are safe for your little one, check for any parts that may come off and become a choking hazard, as well as toxins, such as toxic paints. Inevitably your little champ tries to put all toys (and most other things) into her mouth, so make sure toys you're providing are safe to put in her mouth.

Other accessories

You find most of these things lurking in homes where kids live:

>> **Baby bath or tummy tub:** You need something to wash your baby in and most parents go with a traditional tub that you can have on a table or sturdy bench. Using a smaller tub means you don't have to fill up a normal-sized tub and break your back leaning down into it. While your baby is still really small and unable to sit up by herself, having a bath support can be handy. A bath support is a ramp that baby can lie back on that holds her at a 45-degree angle so her head is safely kept out of the water. Another option for bathing is to use a tummy tub, which looks a bit like a wastepaper basket but is said to replicate being in the womb. Baby 'sits' upright in it and is held snugly in place by the tub's walls. Tummy tubs are pricey, though, so shop around.

>> **Bouncinette or baby chair:** Most kids have spent time in a bouncinette — those ramp-like baby chairs that bub can lie in and watch you go about your day from a better angle than lying on the floor. They're portable, easy to clean and she can even sit outside in one while you're gardening or pegging out washing.

>> **Highchair:** When bub starts solids, you're going to need somewhere she can sit and be fed. A wide range of highchair models is available, from chairs with an ergonomic design made of timber that hasn't been treated with chemicals to chairs with more levers and straps than a space shuttle. Having a detachable tray that you can take off and clean regularly (after every meal!) is handy, as are safety straps so you can be sure bub isn't going to wriggle her way out and get hurt. As an alternative to a highchair, you may want to use a model that attaches to your table. Later on, you can use little booster seats that you strap to a normal chair.

Take a look at Chapter 8 for information about bathing your new-born baby.

IN THIS CHAPTER

» **Watching your partner transform in the second trimester**

» **Making sense of the medical stuff**

» **Helping your partner during the golden trimester**

» **Understanding what your baby is up to**

» **Preparing your home for your baby's arrival**

Chapter **4**

The Second Trimester

The morning sickness is waning, your partner is feeling a little less exhausted and she's beginning to show a bit of a bump — welcome to the second trimester. Weeks 13 to 28 are usually the best period of pregnancy. You start to see your partner's body change as the baby grows, and feel the baby's first kicks by putting your hand on her belly — a pretty amazing feeling.

REMEMBER

Because 80 per cent of miscarriages happen in the first 12 weeks, many parents don't announce they're pregnant until the second trimester.

In this chapter, I take you through the second trimester, providing insight into what might be happening with your partner and what your baby is up to on the inside.

Enjoying the Golden Trimester

If everything is going well, most pregnant women feel a lot better throughout the second trimester. As your partner's belly is getting bigger, the reality that you're going to have a child really sets in. Exciting times! Towards the end of the second trimester, your partner probably also starts feeling those first kicks and bumps. Typically, this happens around 18 to 20 weeks. Kicks may be hard to spot at first, as that little foot tries to get in touch with you through all those abdominal muscles, but feeling them for the first time is a pretty magic moment.

You see your partner transform as the baby grows, and she may start planning what to buy (not more clothes!) and how to decorate the baby's room. This is called the 'nesting instinct' and you pretty much have to go with it. When purchasing things for the baby, however, dads are hugely important because we tend to 'keep it real'. Many household budgets are under a lot of pressure when the baby arrives and with your partner at times high on hormones, going shopping together can help avoid a local financial crisis.

REMEMBER

Navigating your communication around budgetary issues is likely to be a source of conflict, so tread carefully. Yes, you need to pay the rent or your mortgage and you need to eat, but don't ever let money become more important than your relationship and the reasonable desires and instincts of your partner. (See Chapter 3 for an overview of what you actually need to buy.)

Around 20 weeks, your midwife, obstetrician or GP may send you for an ultrasound scan to make sure the baby's bits are all in the right place and that things are progressing smoothly. If you can't wait another 20 weeks to discover the baby's gender, you can usually find out at this scan — unless junior has those legs crossed! Again, don't feel like this is compulsory. Some people love the gender reveal early, but some equally passionate people say you should wait and savour the surprise at the birth. Either way is fine, so don't be afraid to go your own way on this regardless of what others say.

REMEMBER

Sex during pregnancy is absolutely okay and apparently is even good for the baby as well. Bonus! The second trimester might be the best time to share a bit of passion, although how your partner is feeling throughout pregnancy greatly affects the mood. Stick with consent as your marker and, if you're lucky, the sparks will be flying. If you both feel good about it, pregnancy sex can be a lot of fun. And having sex almost up until labour is not out of the question, depending on how your partner feels. Couples have been known to use sex to bring on labour.

Understanding Medical Stuff

In the second trimester, your caregiver starts to feel for the baby at each check-up by asking your partner to lie down. They also use a *Doppler* or a foetal heartbeat monitor to listen for the baby's heartbeat, which at a remarkable 120 to 160 beats per minute makes it sound like a dance party's going on in there. Your caregiver also checks the *fundal height*, or the length of the uterus as it progresses into the abdomen.

Your midwife, obstetrician or GP may also routinely ask your partner for a urine sample to check for protein in her urine. Blood pressure also gets the once over because high blood pressure combined with protein in urine are indicators of pre-eclampsia.

Now is also the time to ask about a *nuchal fold test* to check for potential birth defects, especially if your partner is older than 35. A nuchal fold test aims to determine the likelihood of your baby being born with *Down Syndrome*. This can be a big issue to consider with significant ethical and psychological ramifications. Talk with your partner about what it would mean, either way, and make sure you do all you can to be aligned on your decisions here.

REMEMBER

Having a child with any kind of disability or abnormality presents challenges you never saw in your future — it will literally change your life — but many parents who experience this say it changed them for the better in ways they never could have imagined. Others' judgment is irrelevant in situations like this. It's your family, and it's between you and your partner.

Choosing a carer

You find a maze out there of midwives, birthing centres, doulas, obstetricians and hospitals. Knowing who does what can help you decide where you would like your baby to be born, and what kind of care you would like to receive during and immediately after birth.

Here's a rundown of the types of carers you can choose between:

>> **GPs** are your general family doctor. They aren't specialists in antenatal care or childbirth, but in rural settings, they can work with the local hospital to provide maternity care.

>> **Midwives** are trained health professionals who give antenatal care, deliver babies, help establish breastfeeding and stick around for up to four to six weeks after the birth to help when you're unsure about your baby's health and wellbeing. Midwives can also ensure the recovery of mums to a healthy state. Midwives take a holistic approach to pregnancy and birth, and often counsel you as a family, acknowledging not just the physical challenges of becoming new parents, but also the importance of your mental and social wellbeing. They see pregnancy and birth as a natural process, not a medical one, and can sometimes deliver your baby at home. While they're trained in their field, midwives aren't doctors and don't perform *caesareans* or prescribe medication (although they can prescribe some specialist drugs). If you choose to go with a midwife and complications arise during the pregnancy or birth, the midwife most likely arranges for you to see an obstetrician in the public health system.

>> **Doulas** are trained supporters who assist your partner before, during and after the birth. They're kind of like a non-medical bestie for your partner — someone who will advocate for her when things fire up during labour. Their job is not to replace a midwife or obstetrician, but to be there to support your partner to have a comfortable labour. They also help with practical aspects such as setting up the home to provide a great environment for bubba, and assist with the emotional adjustment that comes with the arrival of your baby.

>> **Obstetricians** are doctors who specialise in *obstetrics*, or the health of women and babies during pregnancy, birth and after the birth, called the *postpartum* or *postnatal* period. They generally work in hospitals and are often the choice of couples experiencing complications during pregnancy, or who have had trouble getting pregnant. If you choose to use an obstetrician as your carer, you have to pay for it. And it can be costly. In Australia, some of the fees can be claimed back through a Medicare rebate.

During the birth, midwives or hospital nurses are on hand to monitor your baby's progress, but the obstetrician arrives only for the late stages and delivery itself. You may have heard stories describing how an obstetrician only showed up *after* the baby was born. These stories can leave some parents wondering if they might be paying a lot for nothing. This isn't the case. Obstetricians are primarily concerned with the physical health of the baby and mother, and don't help you with any non-medical baby care issues after birth. For example, they won't come to your house to show you how to best change your little nipper's nappy.

TIP

I strongly recommend looking around for a birth and labour coach (such as a doula) who believes in empowering dads to better support their partners during labour. Most antenatal courses that are hospital run (see Chapter 5) cover the basics but are fairly neutral on how dad can be a great support. But some people provide powerful strategies for helping mum through labour — while also giving great guidance for dads who want to be an active support rather than a yawning, nervous appendage who stands around like an idiot feeling guilty and inadequate and waiting for it all to end. Do your homework on this. Finding such a carer and coach may end up being one of the most rewarding investments you'll make in your life.

REMEMBER

Talk with whoever you choose as your maternity carer about the options for where your baby can be born: at home, in hospital or in a birthing centre. The availability of birthing options depends on where you live and the carer you have.

Take time to find the right maternity carer for you. As well as getting referrals from your GP, a good place to start is with recommendations from your friends and colleagues. Make sure you're really happy with your carer and that you've got 'good chemistry'. Things can get pretty hectic during pregnancy or birth, so make sure you're in good hands and you're comfortable with your carer's personal and professional style. If you're not happy with your carer, consider changing. Both of you must be 100 per cent comfortable with your choice of carer.

CHECK
THE NET

To find out what services and carers are available in your area, check out www.healthdirectory.com.au. To find a private midwife, go to www.midwivesaustralia.com.au/women/find-a-midwife and to find a doula go to findadoula.com.au.

Birth options

Although the big day is still a few months away, you might want to do a bit of fact-finding around options for giving birth. Getting your baby out of her body is top of mind for your partner and she may have already read up on birth options . . . but rather than getting second-hand information from her, put some time into finding out for yourself.

Just like with parenting philosophies and techniques for getting your baby to sleep, how to give birth is another hot spot for debate among parenting experts (or anyone with an opinion). Suggestions range from home births to elective caesareans.

You don't need to know about all of the various options, but being familiar with key aspects helps. Key concerns mainly come down to the method used for pain relief and the choices for where to have a baby.

The most common options for pain relief during labour are

>> **Drug-free:** Heat packs, massage, breathing exercises and being in water may help relieve the pain of labour. Keeping active during the birth and avoiding lying on her back can also help your partner manage the pain.

>> **Epidural:** An epidural is a local anaesthetic injected into the spinal column. This method of pain relief blocks out all pain and is often used during caesareans so the mother can be awake when her child is born.

>> **Gas:** A mix of laughing gas or nitrous oxide and oxygen has been used for decades and is a safe way to relieve pain during labour. It sometimes makes women feel a bit nauseous.

>> **Pethidine:** A strong pain reliever, pethidine can cause drowsiness in both mother and baby, though usually without any long-term effects. Pethidine can also cause nausea.

Typical options for where and how to have the baby include

>> **Birth centres or free-standing birth centres:** Having your baby in a special birth centre run by midwives might provide you with additional options to try particular birthing techniques or varying positions during labour. However, birth centres generally take a non-interventionist approach and don't provide epidurals.

>> **Home birth:** This option has become more popular. You need the support of a community or private midwife. If your partner wants a water birth, you can hire special equipment to facilitate the birth at home. (Using your existing bath will be impractical — kinda squishy in there.)

>> **Hospital birth:** Most women in Australia opt for a hospital birth. Some hospitals provide extra facilities for water births or natural (as in no pain relief) births.

See Chapter 5 for more on choosing a birth option that's right for you and deciding on a birth plan.

REMEMBER

Talk with your carer about your options and discuss the pros and cons of each one. Don't be afraid to ask questions and be sure you know everything you need to be confident about the upcoming birth. As your partner's number one support person, you need to know what's going on just as much as she does.

TIP

Your birth option may also depend on whether you go through the public health system or use private health insurance. In many states in Australia, home birth is available only for low-risk pregnancies and through private health care.

Dealing with Common Side Effects in the Second Trimester

Most changes during this trimester are a result of the growing size of your baby. They include

>> **Back pain:** This is perhaps one of the most common complaints of pregnant women and is caused by the growing weight of the baby, additional strain on the spine and a change in the centre of gravity that the body needs to adjust for.

>> **Constipation:** Yup, it's a shocker but your partner may find it hard to 'go'. The main reason for constipation in the second trimester is an increase in the hormone progesterone, which slows the movement of food through the digestive tract. Later in pregnancy, the problem of constipation is likely to be made worse by the pressure of the growing uterus on the intestines. Taking iron supplements, which many pregnant

women need, can also make constipation worse. Talk to your GP or a dietician for the safe solutions.

>> **Heartburn:** This burning sensation in the middle chest is caused by the hormone progesterone, which softens the uterus so it can stretch, but also softens the oesophagus, allowing acid to come back out. So if your partner complains about heartburn, don't be offended — your cooking isn't the cause.

>> **Leg cramps:** These seem to plague pregnant women more at night, but no-one's sure what causes them. Blame the hormones, I reckon.

>> **Softening ligaments:** The ligaments in the pelvis stretch, which widens the pelvis to prepare for birth. Softening ligaments can give your partner a floating sensation in the joints and cause sharp stabbing pains when she stands up too quickly or rolls over in bed. This is called *round ligament pain* and is nothing to be worried about, although knowing about this pain is good.

You can't do much about the ailments outlined in the preceding list, other than continue to be a superstar with your support, love and encouragement.

Finding Out What Your Baby's Up To Now

At 24 weeks, your baby is about 21 centimetres from head to bottom (see Figure 4-1). He also has his calendar full doing these amazing things:

>> **Getting his eyes done:** Pigmentation in the iris develops. If your baby is of European descent, he's born with blue eyes that may change colour in the months after birth. Maori, Aboriginal, African, Indian, Pacific Island and Asian babies can be born with brown or blue eyes, and eye colour can also change with time.

>> **Having a facial:** Your baby's using the world's best moisturiser, *vernix*, a waxy coating that keeps his skin from getting wrinkled as he floats around in fluid all day. He also grows fingernails, hair and eyebrows.

>> **Listening to music and your voice:** Your baby can hear now, but won't know what he's hearing for a long time yet — though research suggests that babies know their parents' voices when they're born from what they hear in the womb. Amazing, isn't it?

>> **Preparing to rock and roll:** At the end of the second trimester, your baby is almost done growing and developing all external and internal organs.

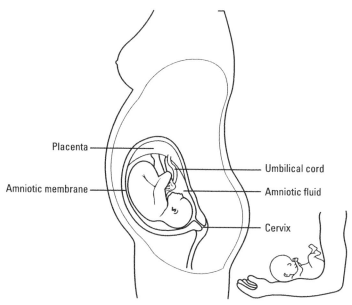

Placenta

Amniotic membrane

Umbilical cord

Amniotic fluid

Cervix

FIGURE 4-1: At 24 weeks, your baby is about the length from your elbow to your wrist.

Making Room for the Baby

When you were growing up, do you remember how important having your own room or separate space was? Your baby's room is more than the place where his bed is, or where his clothes are stored. It's a child's sanctuary, his own special space that has all the things he loves close by. Although he won't know this for a wee while yet, you can start creating that individual, happy space for him before he's born. But first I cover what you need to have.

The nursery

Cot, bassinet, drawers, change table, rocking chair, bookshelves, toy boxes — the nursery is one place you can spend a whole bunch of money on all new stuff if you're not careful. Here are some of the basic items you need to set up a nursery.

Somewhere to sleep

For the first few months, most bubs sleep in a bassinet or Moses basket. A bassinet is like a basket on legs. If the bassinet is on wheels, you can move it from room to room easily during the day for naps (babies can sleep anywhere when they're newborns) and wheel it into either your room or the nursery at night. When your little one has outgrown the bassinet, he can graduate to a cot, where he sleeps until he's about two, or has worked out how to climb out of it.

If you're getting a second-hand cot or bassinet, check it thoroughly to make sure nothing can fall apart and injure your baby. To find out more about ensuring your baby's safety when sleeping and reducing the risk of SUDI (sudden unexplained death of infants), check out Chapter 9.

Somewhere to be changed and dressed

A lot of nurseries have change tables — tables at the right height so you don't have to lean a lot to change bub's nappies or get him dressed. Some experts advocate that babies should be changed on the floor to avoid having baby roll off a change table, but others just stand by the rule that baby is never left on the table unsupervised — even for a second. Whichever you choose, having a change mat or a load of cloth nappies to have under him to catch any rogue pees and poos is essential.

TIP

Cloth nappies are an essential accessory — and not only for covering your baby's bum. They can act as change mats, be put over your shoulder to catch any baby spew when you're burping him, be put on the floor during nappy-free time to catch any accidents and can be slung over the handle of a baby capsule to act as a sun shade. They're inexpensive, washable, very hardy and every nappy bag should have one. See Chapter 5 for more on the pros and cons of using them for their intended purpose — as nappies.

Somewhere to store clothes

You would think that so small a person wouldn't need much room for his clothes, but he grows so big so fast he needs room to store not only the clothes he currently fits, but also the ones he grows into. Hand-me-downs and presents from well-meaning friends and family usually mean clothes are rarely in short supply. Child-sized hangers for his wardrobe can be bought from a homeware or discount store.

TIP

If you're given too many hand-me-down clothes, having a system in place for sizing stops you feeling overloaded. Have designated boxes for each size and store them in your baby's wardrobe. As your baby grows out of one size, you've got another size ready to go. This is a great job for dad when your partner feels like she has too much on her plate — and too many hormones whizzing around — during pregnancy or after birth.

Bits and bobs

Other things that are handy to have include

>> A nappy bucket with tight-fitting lid for soaking soiled clothing, bedding and cloth nappies. Although baby poo doesn't smell at first, it gets smellier as your baby gets older — so this is a useful investment!

>> A rocking chair or armchair where mum can breastfeed or you can give the last bottle of the day before bed. An armchair or rocking chair is also somewhere to share stories, songs and cuddles as your baby gets bigger. Some mums find chairs without arms most comfortable, so have a few options available for your good lady.

>> A pedal rubbish bin with a lid — big size if you're using disposable nappies. Yes, the pedal is essential!

>> Something to house toys and books, such as a bookshelf or toy box.

>> A lockable medicine box where you store health items, such as pain relief, a thermometer and nail clippers.

Chapter 5 has more information about consumables you need for your newborn.

Decorations

Decorating your baby's room is another way to clean out your wallet in a hurry, because thousands of things are available to put in a little person's room. Expectant mums can be tempted to get carried away, so you may have to work together to establish your shopping rationale.

Babies spend a lot of time gazing into space when they're really small, as if they're tuning into a radio show you can't hear, and like looking at high-contrast objects around them, such as black and white shapes. Keep the decorating simple. As your baby develops his taste and his needs change, transforming the nursery into a little child's room won't be a drama.

Here are some tips for keeping your decorations simple:

>> Keep the colours neutral, so that the room can easily be redecorated as your baby grows. Use colours with a very light and calming shade — so that your baby isn't constantly alarmed by the fire engine red on the walls, for example.

>> Use pictures of close friends and family on the walls so your baby can grow up knowing who the important people are.

>> You or your partner may want to make something special for the baby's room, like a painting or piece of embroidery.

>> Mobiles hanging from the ceiling don't need to be fancy. A string of shells hanging from driftwood can entertain a newborn baby for hours.

>> Use removable decals on the walls, so they can be easily taken off as bub grows up and won't damage the wallpaper or paint.

>> Involve your child in the decoration of his room as he gets older. After all, his room is his space.

Animals in the house

A few years ago, you may have bought a puppy or kitten when you and your partner were first thinking about having a baby, but weren't quite ready to take the plunge. Now that your real baby is on the way, you need to think about what's happening to the pets in your house. Your pet is likely to find itself a long way down the pecking order once your cherub is on the scene, and having to put up with pulled fur, fingers in eyes and other orifices, and being chased and ridden.

While this is not so necessary with a newborn, you'll want to keep in mind that kids aren't always wise in the way they approach and respond to animals. Once they're big enough, show your child how to be gentle with animals and people from the get-go, as well as how to approach dogs with caution. A child should always hold his hand out for a dog to smell and stay still when it comes near so the dog doesn't see him as a threat.

Teach your child not to touch strange animals (almost impossible until he's a bit older) and to wash his hands afterwards because animals can carry all sorts of nasties in their fur.

Don't leave your child alone or out of sight with pets. Cats can react badly when your baby decides it's time to 'ride the kitty' and may even give junior a scratch or two. If the mantra of being gentle to the cat doesn't warn your child that felines aren't to be messed with, then a scratch on the nose most certainly will. In the early days it's all about one thing: keeping the pets away from the newborn. Keep them out of baby's room (and cats out of your baby's cot). The idea that cats will purposely try to smother your baby is a myth, but animals can be unpredictable and you need to be sure your little one is safe.

REMEMBER

Dogs and cats can feel neglected when a new baby joins the family, so spend time making them feel settled and happy. Don't move your pet's special sleeping areas or toys away to make room for baby. Try to keep your pet's routines as settled as possible so it doesn't feel left out.

IN THIS CHAPTER

» Finding out what mum and baby are up to in the third trimester

» Deciding on your birth plan

» Checking your baby's progress with tests and check-ups

» Helping your partner get through the third trimester

» Shopping for your baby's needs

Chapter **5**

The Third Trimester

Three is a lucky number, so shouldn't the third trimester be the best of them all? In a way, the third trimester is the best because you end up with your newborn baby, but the period can feel like quite hard work for your partner (and that's even before labour starts).

During this last trimester, your baby has to grow a lot. As a result, your partner's belly gets quite big and a few everyday tasks become quite tricky. You're likely to be busy with all sorts of preparations for the baby's arrival in your house and with preparations for 'B Day'.

In this chapter, I run through what you need to know about birth plans, what your baby is up to and what consumables your baby needs after she's arrived.

Getting through the Third Trimester — Are We There Yet?

The good news is you're on the final lap now. Don't get too excited, though — you still have some hoops to jump through. You may have to go the extra mile during this trimester to support your partner, because things get decidedly uncomfortable for many mums towards the end of their pregnancy. Help with whatever she's asking you to do and put on a brave face. (No whining and moaning allowed — hey, would you want to swap places?)

Now's the time to find out about childbirth or antenatal classes. Childbirth education is the perfect place to find out everything you ever wanted to know about giving birth, and your partner is likely to love you even more for taking an interest. To some, childbirth classes may seem like a bit of a drag, but they're actually quite useful in terms of educating yourself (quickly) about the process of birth. Most importantly, you're able to ask some tricky questions, perhaps meet parents who have just had a new baby, and share tall tales about pregnancy and birth with other dads.

TIP

Most childbirth educations programs focus primarily on the birth process and the drug options your partner will have at her disposal, along with the support provision the birth facility provides. But if you look around, you can often find private providers who offer information that really goes above and beyond, helping you to be the best support you can for your partner, and offering her solutions and strategies that are safe alternatives to the standard medical practices that many modern mums are unsure about.

Attending childbirth classes is also a great way to build a support network because lots of people go on to keep in touch with their antenatal classmates as their babies grow.

A range of public and private providers of childbirth classes exist in Australia. If you're having your baby at a hospital, check if they provide antenatal classes. Ask your carer, check with Medicare or speak to your friends or colleagues who have already been to one.

TIP

Checking with someone who has already attended an antenatal class you're interested in is definitely a good idea. Some classes are more dad-inclusive than others. For example, some providers split the group into mums and dads to talk about specific issues or situations. Having a guys-only session as part of an antenatal class is great because it provides the ideal opportunity for some 'man talk' about pregnancy, babies and fatherhood.

REMEMBER

The right classes and instructors will show you how you can be way more than a worried, tired appendage. Instead, you can be genuinely and supportively involved in the birth, and it will bring you both closer together.

The Birth Plan

The time's come to start looking forward to The Birth. That baby is going to have to come out. In ye olde days, birth involved fewer choices — woman goes into labour, sheets are torn into strips, water is boiled, a lot of yelling occurs, and then (hopefully) baby comes out safely. Of course, birth in those distant times was far from straightforward — it was a dangerous time and both infant and maternal mortality were frighteningly high.

These days, significant risks still exist for mum and bub, but with our technology and greater awareness of the anatomy of birth, the risks are greatly reduced. On the flip side, you're faced with a lot of choices concerning how junior enters the world. Home birth or hospital birth? No drugs, or all the drugs you can get? With lots of family, a video camera and updates on Twitter? Or just your partner, the person delivering the baby and you?

Fortunately, the modern world has also come up with an answer to organise all the various options you may want to consider — a *birth plan*. This sounds like an oxymoron, because birth is generally a natural process that you just have to surrender to — more often than not, you have very little control over what happens. But you can still have preferences.

A birth plan is not like a formal contract and may not even be recorded in written format. Most likely, you simply discuss the various pain relief options and delivery methods with your midwife, obstetrician or GP. Your carer can tell you about pros and cons for each option and you can tell your carer which option you're keen on and which you're not. So a birth plan is really just stating your preferences — providing a clear understanding of how you would like things to go so that the person delivering your baby knows your wishes.

REMEMBER

Keep an open mind about how the birth may go. If you've planned for a nice water birth at home, be prepared that, if things don't go as smoothly as you would like, you may have to be transferred to hospital. Or, if you've said absolutely no way is my woman going to need pain relief, she may be yelling for an epidural in the first five minutes. (And let's be clear — it's not for you to be saying what her pain relief decisions will be. It's up to her. Let it go . . . or tie a rope to your testicles and let her strangle the rope every time a contraction hits — and don't think about even taking a Panadol to reduce the pain.) The ultimate aim is delivering your baby safely into the world with the least amount of anxiety and trauma for your beloved so you set off on your parenting path on the healthiest and safest foot.

REMEMBER

If you've decided on a hospital birth, check out your options (if you have several hospitals in your area to choose from) because standards and facilities vary significantly. Most hospitals offer special 'tours' for pregnant couples to see what the facilities are like and where you need to go on B-Day. This tour is really useful because you can check out details and take lots of time to ask everything you ever wanted to know about giving birth in a hospital.

Understanding More Medical Stuff

As you head into the home stretch of pregnancy, you have more frequent check-ups with your midwife, obstetrician or GP. Your doula, if you have one, may become more involved.

The checks generally involve examining the baby's position and making sure she's in the right place. During this trimester, your baby usually makes her way down head first towards the cervix ready for birth, a process called *engaging*. If she has her feet pointed down towards the cervix, she's in a *breech* position. If she stays breech until the birth, your carer may recommend a caesarean birth.

Your caregiver may also take swabs from your partner's vagina to test for *group B strep*, which is a bacteria that can infect your baby as she's being born. If traces of it are discovered, your carer may recommend your partner is put on an antibiotic drip during labour.

For all the medical stuff you need to know about labour, check Chapters 6 and 7.

Dealing with Common Side Effects in the Third Trimester

By now, the golden glow of the second trimester has often mostly vanished. As your partner nears her due date, your baby is starting to take over her body — literally. Her internal organs are getting pushed and shoved all over the place and her abdominal muscles have split in the middle to make way for that wide load she's carrying. Your partner may even waddle a little, as her relaxed ligaments widen her pelvis.

Some common complaints during this time include the following:

>> **'I've got baby brain':** Pregnant women often feel like they're losing their marbles. They tend to forget stuff, or get a bit vague even during simple or frequent activities. These symptoms are believed to be caused by hormones, lack of sleep and the general toll pregnancy takes on the body. Be patient and compassionate. We blokes can't even conceive of what this does to a woman's body and life.

>> **'I can't sleep but I'm so tired all the time':** Insomnia is one thing most mothers-to-be in the third trimester agree on. Her joints may be sore and back aching, with a baby that kicks all night and heartburn to boot. Your partner may also need to get up for a wee every five minutes. Lying on her back to sleep can put pressure on the *vena cava*, an important artery feeding the heart, so she has to lie on her side at night, and turning over in bed can be a little trying. You can suggest she try a pillow under her right side, where the vena cava is, which tilts the weight of her body off the artery. But mostly just be patient and compassionate.

>> **'I've got varicose veins, and worse — piles':** The third trimester can be hard on your partner. She's getting rounder by the day, can't be as active as she's used to, she's tired, and not getting enough sleep is making her grumpy. Stretch marks are likely appearing on her pregnant belly. And then haemorrhoids — also known as piles — turn up and make her feel downright miserable. She's likely not feeling like a radiant mother-to-be anymore — and may even be feeling like a veiny, fat frump. Varicose veins and piles can be caused or made worse by the weight of the baby on her body, so help her to take it easy and rest lots.

>> **'My ankles are swollen and I'm as big as a house':** As well as carrying a rapidly growing baby around, your partner's retaining fluid and has more blood flowing through her body. In hot weather or after standing for long periods, this blood collects in her ankles. Your partner should put her feet up whenever she can and avoid salty foods. A few foot rubs from dad wouldn't go amiss, either. Calling her 'huge' or 'ready to pop' doesn't go down well — ever, under any circumstances — even if you think she looks hilarious. Even if she's laughing along with you, she's probably not laughing.

>> **'Why doesn't anything I eat taste right?':** Blame that pesky progesterone — along with everything else, the hormone causes food cravings. Finding anything that tastes just how she wants it to be may be very hard for your partner, and predicting what she needs is almost impossible. Roll with the cravings and keep up your partner's spirits by getting her whatever she asks for — even if it means a late-night takeaway run for another cheeseburger.

TIP

Taking walks together, reading or singing to the baby in bed at night, making lists of potential names together, and taking photos of that burgeoning belly make for a good time and help you support each other as the big day approaches. These are some of the last days that your family numbers just the two of you, so take time to be with your partner right now.

Finding the Right Consumables

A whole aisle of the supermarket is dedicated to baby stuff for a reason — your baby needs a lot of baby-specific things on a regular basis and a lot is available to choose from. Parents also make for really easy prey for marketing people. A few sleepless nights and sheer desperation does amazing things to your shopping habits. So having a good nosey round all the stuff you can buy before the baby arrives makes the shopping-in-a-hurry experience easier on you later on. Don't worry about buying the wrong nappy cream, teething gel or nappies. You go through lots of them and have plenty of opportunities to try out different options. But the following sections help you get a head start.

Nappies

As proper blokes, we don't think about nappies, of course. Until we become dads, that is. Get used to nappies . . . they become your friends, because they're between you and a whole lot of pee and poo.

You can select from three main options when choosing what to wrap your baby's bottom in — cloth nappies that can be washed and used over and over, disposable nappies that you throw away after each change, and hybrids where you throw away some bits and wash and re-use the main bit.

Of course, you can aim for nappy-free and practise *elimination communication*, if that's your thing (see Chapter 8).

Cloth nappies have come of age. No longer are cloth nappies those scratchy, leaky, bulky cloth things that require a degree in origami to fold into the right shape and are held together with safety pins. Now cloth nappies come already shaped with domes and Velcro to make putting them on and getting them off as easy as a disposable nappy.

CHECK THE NET

Australia's Clean Cloth Nappies (cleanclothnappies.com) provides information on how to use and wash cloth nappies. You can also check out the Australian Nappy Association (www.australiannappyassociation.org.au), which represents cloth nappy manufacturers and promotes cloth nappy use.

Cloth nappies do require a bit more money upfront and require time and energy washing them, and you have to be willing to literally get your hands dirty. But some comparisons show cloth nappies to come out cheaper than disposables. Modern cloth nappies can also be used on more than one child and can be bought in good condition secondhand. Eco-conscious dads can rest assured your child's nappies aren't clogging up landfills for years to come.

WARNING

But if you think just changing a nappy is gross, having to clean them may be a step too far for you. Up until this point in your life, you've probably avoided getting too much crap on your hands. Cloth nappies need cleaning. Manually. You can't just stick that dirty stink bomb in the washing machine without giving it a scrub first — and, for some, that's asking too much.

Disposable nappies mean you never have to clean a nappy. They can be a better option if you're on holiday, or for use in the day-to-day nappy bag — so if your baby needs a change when you're out and about, you don't have to carry a dirty nappy around until you get home. A handful of eco-friendly disposable nappy brands are on the market in Australia. They're available in most supermarkets at comparable prices to the major brands. They're typically made from corn starch and other sustainable resources, and often don't contain any of the chemicals that keep babies dry but which may cause nappy rash, as well as being bad for the environment. All in all, a sound alternative.

Hybrid nappies are made of a washable underpants part and a disposable pad. Hybrid nappies generally require upfront investment in the pants, but tend to work out cheaper in the long run.

TIP

Disposable nappies may be right for you if you live in an area where water is scarce. Cloth nappies use a lot of water in rinsing and washing.

Crème de la crèmes

Nappy rash is a big concern for most babies from time to time. The condition occurs when the ammonia from bub's poos and wees irritates her skin, making it red and tender, and making her pretty unhappy with life. The easiest way to stop nappy rash in its tracks is to change that nappy frequently. But doing so means a lot more nappies, money, work, or all three. Even then, you'll still probably have the issue of nappy rash at some point. A healthy way to reduce nappy rash is to expose the baby's bottom to air and sunlight for a good half an hour each day — but not in the middle of the day when sunburn will be a concern. (No baby wants either nappy rash or a burnt bum.) Using a barrier cream protects her backside from a nasty rash, too.

Like all things baby, you can find an enormous range of nappy creams on the market and your partner might have a few ideas of what to get. Don't feel overwhelmed by the vast choice of products available. At the end of the day, anything from the supermarket that has zinc oxide in it does the trick. Castor oil and zinc oxide cream is very effective and cheap, but it can be thick and sticky, so you might want to use it at night and have a lighter cream in the day, or use a powder with zinc oxide in it. You can also try out Vaseline as a barrier cream.

Manufacturers want you to buy all sorts of other creams to make your little champ smell good, have nice skin, be more successful in life, fall asleep better and so on. By all means, try them out and, if you find one that works really well, keep using it. In general, I recommend keeping your choices simple and using natural oils, which are cheap and effective. Olive or almond oil have been known to be particularly effective for most temporary skin irritations and even cradle cap (see following section).

Shopping for your baby's health and first aid

Having an arsenal of potions and lotions on hand in the early months and years is essential. Here's what every dad should have in his baby fix-it kit:

- » **Almond or calendula oil:** Your baby doesn't need moisturisers or scented lotions. If she has dry skin, pure oil is best because it doesn't have all the toxins and fillers big companies use to preserve their products. Calendula oil is really great for massage, and almond oil is great for dry skin and *cradle cap*, a condition common in babies where flakes form on the scalp like baby dandruff.

- » **Antibacterial cream:** Stop infections in cuts and grazes by treating them with antibacterial cream.

- » **Arnica cream:** As she grows, your baby is going to get her fair share of bumps on the head and knees. Arnica cream applied to the bruise can assist with the healing.

- » **Child's sunscreen and insect repellent:** Essential if you live in tropical climes, but the best form of protection is clothing and keeping out of the sun. Babies' skin is a lot more sensitive than adults' skin so junior can burn even when she's not exposed to direct sunlight. Mosquito nets can be bought to go over the cot or bassinet, too.

- » **Digital thermometer:** If your baby is sick with a cold or flu, you can tell when to whip her off to the doctor by using a digital thermometer to check her temperature. Take your baby's temperature by putting the thermometer under her arm and checking what's called the *axillary temperature*. 'Normal' temperature is 37 degrees Celsius. Unfortunately, some babies don't enjoy having a thermometer stuck under their arm for long enough to get an accurate reading. If your little one is like that, you may want to consider getting an ear thermometer, which takes the measurement in seconds.

>> **Karvol, Vicks Baby Balsam and Euky Bearub:** Karvol is a decongestant that can be applied to the baby's clothes to clear nasal passages as she sleeps. Vicks Baby Balsam and Euky Bearub are applied to the chest and back when she's congested. Check these medicines are suitable for your baby's age.

>> **Nail clippers or baby nail scissors:** Babies can scratch themselves easily so you need to keep their nails short and neat. This is easier said than done. Try small nail clippers or special baby scissors to see what works best for you.

>> **Pain reliever:** Children's Panadol (Pamol) or Nurofen for kids is used for pain and fever after immunisations and teething, and fever when your baby has a cold. Use a plastic syringe with measurements marked on the side to dispense the medication and check with your doctor for the correct dosage (which is worked out by baby's weight). Aspirin is not suitable for young children.

>> **Teething relief:** Teething powder and gels such as Bonjela can help soothe a teething baby's gums.

WARNING

Check with your GP before giving your baby pain relief medication if she's younger than six months old. Always check the labelling on any medical product (or any product, in fact) to make sure it's suitable for your baby's age. If you're unsure whether it's suitable — for your baby's age or for the condition you're hoping to treat — check with your GP.

TIP

Be prepared to keep adding to your household first-aid kit with bandages, bandaids, ointments, scissors and tweezers as your little one gets older and encounters more little accidents.

3

The Big Moment is Here: Birth

Understand what's actually going on at each stage and phase of labour.

Find out the medical information you need to know before labour, and keep in mind during what can be quite a drawn-out affair.

Pick up some tips and tricks to help you — and your partner — get through it all.

Know what to do in the first few hours after birth when you finally hold your brand new baby in your arms.

IN THIS CHAPTER

» **Finalising preparations for Project Push**

» **Finding out what happens during labour**

» **Supporting your partner in labour**

» **Sorting out your last-minute items**

» **Understanding when labour really begins**

Chapter **6**

Final Preparations

B eing born is, ironically, the most dangerous thing you probably do in your life. In developing countries, just being born or having a baby is still a precarious thing to do. That said, infant mortality rates are at the lowest in history and constantly dropping. In Australia, problems during birth are rare and plenty of help is available if things get a bit tricky.

But that doesn't mean you can take everything for granted. You need to know what's going on during birth. Knowledge is power, so I've built this chapter to keep you in the loop. Of course, no two births are the same and no-one can tell you what's going to happen during the birth of your child. The process may seem a bit random and very drawn out, but usually that's just part of the journey to dadhood.

In this chapter, you find out about the different phases and stages of labour, when real labour starts and when to call your carer. You discover strategies for making labour less of a pain for your partner and how to keep both of you sane during this trying time.

Making those final arrangements

You have so much to do and only nine months to do it in. Along with watching your partner's belly grow and preparing for the biggest change in your life yet, you can do a whole bunch of things to minimise the chaos in your world right now and to save yourself a bit of hassle down the line. The following sections provide some ideas.

Upskilling

You're only a few weeks or days away from birth and you know everything possible to know about giving birth and newborn baby care (say 'yes'). If not, I'd strongly suggest you enrol yourself in a last-minute antenatal or postnatal course — some of them are done over just one weekend, so you still have time.

CHECK THE NET

If you're short on time or need more flexibility around when you complete your childbirth course, an online option may work best for you. Check out nourishbaby.com.au and their online Guide to a Positive Labour and Birth course. For more about antenatal courses, refer to Chapter 5.

If you want to go beyond upskilling on the basics of baby care and childcare, you can also check out courses that teach baby massage, baby sign language and active movement with babies. (Examples abound on the web of how you can start connecting with your baby from day one.)

Transport

You've no doubt seen movies where Ms Pregnant goes into labour and Mr Pregnant drives like a crazy man to get to the hospital before the baby's born. If you're having a hospital birth rather than a home birth, some variation of the movie scene is likely to happen to you — without the driving like a crazy man part, of course. Instead, you can do some preparation now to help ensure you get there calmly and safely.

Depending on how far away you live, you may want to check some time in advance of the birth how to get to the hospital. Some people even do a test run to see how long the drive takes them — and that's not as over-the-top as it seems. The more familiar you are with exactly where you're going, the more calm you both are on the ride in — and the more you can focus on the things that matter, such as safety and your partner's comfort and contractions.

When you do your hospital tour, ask the staff if any special parking is available for families in the maternity ward. This could save you time — and a long, uncomfortable walk for your partner — when the big moment arrives. Unlike the movies, a parking space isn't likely to magically appear right outside the delivery suite doors (although they likely have a drop-off zone nearby), so doing a little investigative work before the big day about where you can park is worthwhile.

TIP

You might also want to think about the following transport considerations:

>> Is where you park the car at home accessible night and day, or is your car blocked in by other cars at certain periods?

>> If your car doesn't start (think flat battery), do you have someone you can call as a back-up?

>> Do you have enough fuel in the tank to get you there?

>> Have you got a capsule or car seat to transport your baby home? Is it fitted correctly? Do you know how to use it? (That is, take out the capsule to carry the baby, place the capsule into the holder, and so on?)

Birthing equipment for home birth

If you're having a hospital birth, you don't need to bring anything to the delivery suite other than your beloved and her hospital bag (which in some instances can be pretty big indeed). But if you're having the birth at home, you need some bits and bobs to prepare for the big day.

Consider getting the following together if planning a home birth:

>> **A birthing pool:** These can be hired or purchased from private companies or through your local homebirthing association. Some can even be used as a paddling pool for your child afterwards.

>> **A container for the placenta:** By now, you're likely aware that after the baby is born, another process is

required — the delivery of the placenta. Known as the *third stage of labour*, safe delivery of the complete placenta is vitally important for your partner's wellbeing — retained placenta can be fatal. And delivering the placenta can make some mess (because childbirth is messy). Be prepared with somewhere to put it, such as a bucket.

>> **Towels:** For cleaning up and wrapping the baby after birth, and for mum and dad if you've both been in the pool.

>> **Waterproof mats to cover your carpet:** A tarpaulin covered with newspaper and an old blanket or sheets should provide enough protection.

Your midwife can give you a full list of everything you need to have prepared.

The hospital bag(s)

The old conundrum of knowing what to take on holiday and what to leave behind is nothing compared to the quandary of what to take to the hospital when your baby is on its way.

Packing the hospital bag is often broken down into three sections — things needed for mum during the birth, things needed for mum after the birth and things needed for the baby. Things needed for dad often get a bit neglected, because fathers have a little more flexibility and capacity to look after their own needs (if and when those needs arrive).

Chances are you won't be thinking about what you need once the labour kicks off. So in your final preparations and bag packing, focus on the needs of mum and bub.

In the following sections, I outline what to pack in a mum- and baby-friendly hospital bag.

What the parents need during the birth

You need some or all of the following items for the big event:

>> **Appropriate clothing:** Mum's feet might get cold in an air-conditioned hospital, so pack a pair of nice comfy soft socks. Work out what she wants to wear while she is in labour, and make sure it's in the bag — though be aware that clothing becomes an annoyance for many women in

labour, and she may decide to take most of it off. If you're having a water birth or plan to use the shower during labour at the hospital, you might want to pack a pair of shorts so you can get in the pool or shower, too.

>> **Mobile phone and charger:** In this day and age, this almost goes without saying, but I'll say it anyway. Remember your phone charger. Your phone is going to get a workout during these next few days.

>> **Headphones:** In your partner's downtime during recovery, she may want to close out the world and have some quality screen or music time on her phone.

>> **Snacks and drinks:** Some labours can take a long time (24 hours is not unusual), and mum doing all the pushing and dad doing all that supporting is hard work. Hydration and energy are the two things most needed by a labouring mum. To keep fluids up, offer water, juice or ice. Hydration assists the muscles to do their work and they need it.

TIP

The digestion process almost stops as labour progresses. Your partner's body has too many other — and more important — things to focus on rather than digestion, so the easier food is to digest, the better. Easy to digest foods include fruit such as grapes, ripe bananas or whatever is in season, and juices. Pack some snacks for yourself as well — you don't want to be marauding hospital corridors during the night when you're hungry, and the food in the hospital hallway vending machines is not particularly sustaining.

WARNING

Plan to minimise your phone use during labour. Watching Instagram reels or sports on your phone while your partner is in labour doesn't usually go down so well. Instead plan to have your phone turned off most of the time — the main game is what is happening right there in front of you and the more you are 'present', the stronger the connection you will have together. Pain and discomfort are very personal things, but someone being there 'with you' and doing what they can for you is a world away from having them watch something funny on YouTube or grab a sports update.

Your partner likely won't want loud noises or strong smells (such as candles or incense) with her in the birthing room, so no need to pack these.

What mum needs after the birth

In all likelihood, after the birth you ideally spend a few hours with your new baby, call everyone you want to call and feel a little giddy. You probably head home for a shower, something to eat and a sleep. But mum needs at least these things to help her settle into her stay at the hospital:

>> A change of comfortable clothes for coming home — just make sure you don't pack pre-pregnancy clothes, because your partner's body won't usually completely re-adjust straightaway

>> Lanolin nipple cream that doesn't need to be washed off before breastfeeding

>> Maternity bras and nursing pads for leaking breastmilk

>> Maternity pads (though these can be supplied by the hospital)

>> Pen and notebook for recording a few things after the birth

>> Pyjamas or a nightie that opens at the front for breastfeeding, a dressing gown and slippers

>> Soft cotton undies

>> Toiletries your partner uses regularly, such as a toothbrush, shampoos, cleanser, deodorant, moisturiser, lip balm, contact lens supplies, hair bands and brush, and any medications

What bub needs after the birth

The little person you're taking home needs

>> **Disposable nappies:** Even if you're going to use cloth nappies, *meconium*, the sticky tar-like poo your baby expels in the first few days after birth, is best handled by disposable nappies because meconium can be hard to get out of cloth ones. Many hospitals don't give away free nappies anymore, so be prepared and take a few extra.

>> **Bottle feeding equipment (if applicable):** Undoubtedly, breast is best — the empirical research supporting breast-feeding is overwhelming. It's good for mum and it's good for your new baby. But sometimes breastfeeding is not feasible,

and sometimes — even with the best intentions — it just doesn't work out and can't be done. You should feel no shame if this is the case, and in Australia we're fortunate to have an alternative if breastfeeding can't be done. Formula (labelled 'from birth'), bottles, teats and sterilising equipment are all necessary if you're going to bottle feed.

>> **Muslin wraps or blankets:** Hospital air-conditioning can be chilly, and wrapping (or swaddling) your newborn helps him feel more secure.

>> **Something to wear:** A couple of newborn-sized all-in-ones with feet and long sleeves, some hats or beanies, and some socks or booties will also be useful. Newborns are used to being in a nice warm spa pool and aren't great at controlling their temperature yet, so even in summer they need to be kept warm. You may also have a special 'coming home' outfit picked out.

>> **Wipes and nappy rash cream:** These items are needed for cleaning and protecting your baby's bottom while changing her nappies.

WARNING

Don't be tempted to throw in a dummy (or pacifier) when packing for bub. While a dummy is probably one of the most commonly known baby accessories, lactation consultants may not be that happy about you giving your little one a dummy — especially if you're experiencing breastfeeding difficulties. This is because dummies are believed to cause 'nipple confusion' in some cases. Dental experts also argue pretty strongly against them because of the pressure they put on newly formed teeth down the track. Additionally, in a couple of years' time when it's time to ditch the dummy, you're going to find your little baby has a strong opinion about keeping it around. The removal process can get pretty ugly. My advice: avoid a dummy if you can. This may create some short-term pain here and there, but the disadvantages are overwhelming in comparison.

TIP

If you want to go the extra mile to ensure you've got everything you could possibly need for your newborn, check with a midwife. And check with a lactation consultant for any breastfeeding equipment, aids or remedies your partner may need.

GETTING IN ON THE BABY SHOWER

Baby showers being all about mum, where a bunch of women sit around drinking tea and playing games like 'guess what mess is in that nappy', is no longer strictly true. Dads are getting in on the act, too. No, not sitting around eating sandwiches and oohing over Aunty Vera's knitted booties, but getting together to mark your transition into fatherhood. The event could be a game of pool with mates, a day out fishing, a game of tenpin bowling, a joint occasion with mum's mates, or a boys' night out on the town. So by all means, have a 'man shower' or 'daddy shower' to celebrate the occasion. (And, no, your man shower should not replicate anything resembling a stereotypical 'stag' night — if anyone still does them.)

Checklists

In all the excitement of becoming a father, forgetting stuff is really easy, so devise a comprehensive list of everything you think you're likely to need and put this list somewhere you can't miss it. Don't leave getting ready up to your memory — you're bound to forget something.

Your checklist should include

» **Car seat:** Have you got a car seat sorted and know how to fit it into your car?

» **Home birth list:** Mats to protect floors, home birth pool if you want it, towels for yourself and the baby, and anything else your midwife requires.

» **Nursery:** Baby has somewhere to sleep and bedding to sleep in, baby has clothes to wear, you have something to store clothes in, baby has nappies and bum protection, and you have something to change baby on.

» **Pet care:** Who can look after any pets during the birth while you're not at home?

» **Phone list:** Have a back-up list of emergency numbers, and numbers for your lead maternity carer, maternity ward, friends, family and work (as well as having them as contacts on your phone).

>> **Your hospital bags:** For during the birth, for the hospital stay and for bub.

>> **Your transport:** Ensure your car has petrol, you know your way to the hospital, and you know where parking is.

Discovering What You Need to Know about Labour

You can't be too prepared for labour. And because you're number one in the support crew, understanding what's going on is essential. To help you get your head around this momentous occasion and understand what's going on, the Glossary outlines terms used in labour and birth.

You have a lot to take in, so this section provides a guide to what generally happens during labour.

Like all good things in life, labour happens in three stages, as follows:

>> The **first stage** is when your partner's cervix softens, then widens (*dilates*), making space for the baby to transition from the womb (uterus) down the birth canal and out into the world. The uterus contracts at regular intervals (contractions), slowly opening the cervix (the entry to the uterus), which will eventually allow the baby to come through. The contractions become increasingly painful (yes, these are *those* contractions you've heard about and seen in movies). The cervix is fully dilated to allow the baby's birth when it reaches ten centimetres (which is another way of saying the opening from the uterus to the birth canal is wide enough for the baby's head). For a first birth, the first stage takes an average of 6 to 14 hours (but can take a day or more), so you can see that your presence with a strong shoulder, lots of reassurance (and ice to sip), plus heat packs (to soothe) really helps. Not all of this time in the first stage of labour is spent in 'active labour' — more on this later.

>> The **second stage** is the bit where your partner pushes the baby out. The second stage is also helped along by contractions that are different in feeling and intensity to first stage

contractions. Second stage is the stage when mum is actively engaged in pushing the baby out, rather than focusing on 'getting through' the contractions of the first stage — when her job was to relax and let her body do its thing (open her cervix). In the second stage, your partner becomes more actively involved with using each contraction to help your baby come down through the birth canal and out into the world. Second stage is complete when your little one arrives!

>> The **third stage** is a little less glamorous (as if birth is at all glamorous) and involves the placenta, that lifeline to your baby, being born. The placenta is also called *afterbirth*. Delivering the placenta takes between five minutes to an hour. Most women are too knackered by this stage — or energised by finally meeting their baby — to notice much about expelling the placenta. Many births have delivery of the placenta assisted by an injection given into the mother's thigh as the baby's head is birthing at the end of the second stage. This causes the vessels connecting the placenta to the uterine wall to close off and reduces the risk of haemorrhage, so if you see this injection happening, don't be alarmed.

Think that's all there is to it? Nuh-uh. You have a ways to go yet in getting prepared for labour.

REMEMBER

As much as taking in all this information may seem like intense training, it's nothing like the marathon you're going to be part of. The more you understand, the better you are when crunch time comes. Because you understand what is happening in each stage, you can recognise progress and that things are generally following a well-trodden path. Being able to communicate this progress will be a critical support for your partner when the going gets tough. So the more you understand and see the progress, the more you can be that steadying, reassuring influence to your partner and give her the strength to keep going.

The first stage also progresses through three phases. Your partner may be too caught up in the moment to recognise them as they happen to her, but signposts can be spotted along the way. The following outlines the three phases and some of the ways you can identify them:

>> **Latent phase:** This is the very beginning of labour. Contractions begin and are 5 to 20 minutes apart and usually last from 20 to 30 seconds. Generally, these contractions are felt as small waves, often described as moderate tummy cramps. Progression is slow and steady at this stage and continues to be until the cervix is at around three centimetre dilation.

REMEMBER

Life can go on pretty much as normal during the latent phase. If this phase starts at night, don't get caught up timing contractions and watching the clock. Get some sleep. The best thing you (and especially your partner) can do during this phase is to relax, rest, and snooze. If it's happening during the day, just get on with things. (My wife had a haircut while she was in the latent phase of two of our six pregnancies.) All you need to know is that things are starting and that the contractions become more frequent as the labour progresses. (You won't know exactly what the cervix is doing but the contractions indicate when things are revving up.)

>> **Active phase:** This phase is characterised by the cervix dilating from about three centimetres to ten centimetres, known as *fully dilated*. Contractions increase in length and intensity and come every three to five minutes. Your partner is now becoming more inwardly focused. She may be less communicative and doesn't have the headspace to be thinking of what's going on 'out there'. This is where you become 'active' as well — ensuring what she needs is there for her.

TIP

Keep an eye on the timing of these contractions and make sure you're *really present* for your partner through this phase. Be ready with the ice in cups and back rubs. And actively check in, thinking *for* her and providing reassurance — unless she tells you to stop it already!

>> **Transition:** This is the point just before the pushing starts (as part of second stage labour). Contractions are very intense, sometimes overwhelming and your partner may say things like, 'I can't do it!', 'I want this to be overrrr!', 'Get me out of here', or 'I want an epidural!' — plus a whole lot of swear words I don't need to list here. She may also be hot, sweaty, feel nauseous, and make sounds you have never heard before. Remember, this is normal for transition. See the sidebar 'Understanding the drama of transition' for more on why.

UNDERSTANDING THE DRAMA OF TRANSITION

Transition is where the real drama of labour and childbirth occurs. It's the part of labour almost everyone remembers and talks about. Transition doesn't last as long as the other parts of labour (thank goodness), but it is the most memorable in terms of your partner (and you) being taken to the edge. It helps to know why.

As labour progresses, everything will feel pretty smooth, and almost predictable, until transition. Even though the contractions are painful, things will make sense. You'll be timing contractions, and noting what time they each start and how long they are lasting. You'll likely be feeling like things are under control and progressing. And — this is the critical thing — your partner won't be feeling any real urge to push. It's not there. Not a bit. She knows the baby is coming psychologically, and she wants it to happen, but no physical urge is felt yet to actually deliver the baby.

When your partner is dilated to around seven centimetres, a huge shift happens. Until this stage, everything her body has been doing is directed towards her body opening up (dilating). Her cervix has been contracting upwards toward her abdomen — it's literally been pulling *up* the uterus so the opening to the birth canal is wide enough for the baby to pass through safely.

When your partner hits the seven-centimetre dilation mark, her body lifts momentum to a whole new level. Hormones such as oxytocin and endorphins are pumping, and things are picking up in a big way. A transition is taking place — it's almost time for the baby to come down the birth canal and one contraction at this point does the work that many contractions were doing before. It's intense. Only someone experiencing this contraction can understand how it feels — and that's not blokes. So now's the time when you need to be the calm in the storm. This, more than any other time, is the business end of childbirth.

REMEMBER

One of the more obvious signs that things are about to kick off is when your partner's waters break (that is, the membranes of the *amniotic sac* rupture). This sometimes happens in the most inappropriate situation — but, hey, it's all natural. However, your partner's waters breaking doesn't always mean she's in labour.

She may be but, in some cases, labour starts up to 24 hours after the waters break. Either way, calling your midwife or doctor to inform your carer that the waters have broken is a good idea. Read about more signs of the first stage of labour in the section 'When You Think You're in Labour', later in this chapter.

WARNING

If you spot any blood or meconium (poo) when the water breaks, contact your midwife or doctor and seek immediate medical attention.

Understanding Your Role in Labour

Supporting and being there for your partner is really important. So what does 'being there' really mean? Ask a lot of dads who've been through the birth of their children and the answer that might spring to mind is 'Stand around like an idiot and feel guilty and inadequate'. Feeling sidelined is possible when the focus is on your partner and she's in kind of a crabby mood with you — which you would be, too, if you had three kilos of person coming out of an orifice. She's focusing on what her body is doing, listening to the coaching and advice of her midwife or obstetrician, and coping with pain, hormones and emotions you can't even begin to imagine (or don't want to).

In general, your partner relies on you to sort out a long list of support tasks, which you can do with dignity and humility. So, if your partner needs a shoulder to hang onto for leverage when she's pushing, give it to her. If she needs a drink in a cup with a straw and three ice cubes, get it organised. If your partner says she can't do it anymore, tell her with conviction that she can. Being there means taking care of your partner when she needs you to and, most importantly, reassuring her that it will all work out when she needs you to.

REMEMBER

Labour can be totally overwhelming for your partner and she's vulnerable to every emotion in the book. She's also vulnerable to being intimidated by the hospital system: a nurse who suggests pain relief will relax her even though your partner wants to have a natural birth; an obstetrician or midwife who wants to set up a drip to speed things along (and increase stress and pain levels with it) because it might make things go faster but not tell you the downside; or an over pushy *lactation consultant* who's stressing out your exhausted partner. If something doesn't feel right, you have to make a decision for the good of your partner and baby and advocate on their behalf. The health and wellbeing of mum and baby are *always* top of the list, but if the baby isn't showing signs of stress and mum wants to keep trying for the birth you and she have discussed, then give her the encouragement she needs and advocate for her preferences. The decisions involve your family so you get to be 'the man who calls the shots' when push comes to shove.

Dads can really make their role count during labour by being

>> **Thoughtful and connected:** Help out where you can by making sure your partner is as comfortable as she can be, is well stocked with snacks and water, and is warm or cool enough. She may not notice she's thirsty until you offer a drink to her. She may need to be gently prompted to go to the bathroom every 40 minutes or so to empty her bladder. (The walk will help labour along and emptying her bladder will be helpful when the pushing starts — nothing impedes progress like a full bladder.) Gentle reminders with clear direction work best. And be aware of your timing — during the contraction is not the time to suggest anything except that the contraction is doing its work and will be gone soon. (Say things like, 'This is good, and it's helping your body open up. 20 seconds to go. Stay with it. Nearly there.') Once the contraction is over, let her know how well she's done and then suggest what you think she may need. Don't take offence if she shuts down a suggestion — she doesn't have the headspace for small talk. Let her know you have her back and her front and everything else. This is about being there for her and looking out for her when she is at her most vulnerable.

>> **The rational calm voice in the hustle and bustle:** Even when things get stressful or hectic, try to keep your cool on your partner's behalf and advocate for her if things are slipping out of control. Medical staff will be open to requests by you when you are respectful of them. As long as they see what you are asking is in line with what your partner wants, they'll go along with it. A nod from her is always helpful.

>> **A link to the outside world:** Let friends and family know what's going on — because they're likely to be anxious to hear how the birth's going. You can also be the first to announce to the world that your new son or daughter has arrived — a very special thing to be able to do!

REMEMBER

Once labour kicks off, take your cues from your partner. Her needs are pretty specific and she lets you know about them. But don't try to tell your partner you know how she feels, because you don't. Any complaining (to her) of any sort from your end may not be received well, no matter how sore your shoulders and arms are from all that massage or holding her up in the shower.

TIP

Have a standby support person in case labour goes on for a long time, or you desperately need some rest. Talk about who would be suitable with your partner. Perhaps her sister or mother could fill in for you while you have a meal or take a breather.

Getting Ready — Last-Minute Preparations

As you count down the days to your partner's due date, you could be feeling all sorts of things — excitement about meeting your baby for the first time, or absolute terror about the reality of your new responsibility. Anything you're feeling is okay; all expectant dads have been there. You may also be a bit worried about how you're going to handle the birthing process, about your role in it and how well your partner is going to cope. Worrying is okay and, yes, occasionally guys will pass out or throw up during labour, which is all part of the journey. And nearly everyone ends up being emotional — and, yes, crying. Preparing for birth has been a long, hard ride. Having a baby enter the world is a big deal. Basically, just ride it out and remember it doesn't get better than this moment. This is life at its most complete.

Before the fun starts, double-check (or triple-check) a few things, such as ensuring you've

>> Arranged for someone to look after your pets/plants and clear your mail. You may be gone some time.

>> Briefed people at work, or left handover notes or contact details if you need to leave suddenly.

>> Got the hospital bags packed and ready to go, even if you're planning a home birth, in case you need to transfer to a hospital in a hurry.

>> Made sure the car seat is ready to go and practised putting it in and taking it out of the car.

>> Stored phone numbers of friends and family from both sides on your mobile phone and ensured the phone's charged with plenty of credit if you use a prepaid model. (Remember to take your phone charger with you when you leave the delivery room.)

The checklists earlier in this chapter can help you remember anything you may have forgotten.

When You Think You're in Labour

You can have the following signs that the birth of your baby is not far away, but it can be days or weeks before full-on labour really starts.

Here are some indicators that things are about to get interesting, but you shouldn't get too excited yet:

>> **A bloody show or mucous plug:** Most people simply call this 'the show'. The mucous plug that blocks the cervix during pregnancy comes away, along with blood from broken capillaries in the cervix.

>> **Braxton Hicks contractions:** These are mild contractions, similar to strong period pain or cramps. They're not 'real' contractions, but may be confused with them.

>> **Intense or increasing back pain:** This can also be a sign that things are beginning to happen.

>> **Loose bowel motions:** A few days before labour, the body releases prostaglandins, which help soften the cervix ready for dilation. Prostaglandins also cause things to be a bit loose in the bowel department.

Don't worry if none of the things in the preceding list happens before the contractions start. Every labour, birth and woman is different, so call your carer if you're not sure about what's happening.

When the first stage of labour begins, your partner may feel like birth is really happening, but it isn't yet. The difference between the latent phase (also sometimes called *early labour*) and the active phase (sometimes called *active labour*) of the first stage of labour is the length and intensity of contractions. If you're still a bit confused about the various stages and phases of labour, check the definitions provided in the section 'Discovering What You Need to Know about Labour', earlier in this chapter.

If you and your partner aren't sure whether labour has commenced, or whether your partner is in the latent or active phase, call your midwife, obstetrician or GP for support. Your carer can give you guidance on whether you need to grab the car keys, or if you can settle in for the evening.

When You're Really in Labour

All aboard the roller-coaster — and get buckled in, because you're in for a real treat. The birth of a child happens everywhere around the world thousands of times each day. And you can bet that every birth happening right now is unique. Lucky you — you get to be part of your baby's story right now. The high of seeing a child born is like nothing on Earth — and you're about to meet your own child. How cool is that?

First things first. You know your partner is in labour because

» Contractions are regular (one every 5 minutes), lasting 45 to 60 seconds, and increasing in frequency. (If baby is in the *posterior* position — back against mum's spine — contractions will be a lot less regular, with more back ache and less regularity with the contractions.) How long contractions last and how strong they are is key to knowing things are moving along.

» Contractions are getting longer, stronger and closer together, and your partner may not be able to speak during a contraction.

Time to call your carer or head to the hospital (safely) if you haven't already.

TIP

If your carer hasn't already, alert the maternity ward that you are on your way in (using the number you've already stored in your phone). Let them know what is happening regarding contractions — including length and interval — and how far from the hospital you are so they can be ready for your arrival. Stay calm — your mind will be clearer, and you'll give certainty to your partner, who needs it right now. Plus you'll get there safely.

WARNING

Don't go driving fast or tearing around corners like a Formula One driver — after all, you want to all arrive in one piece at the hospital. This is not the time to be the hero in the car. Fast driving won't make your partner feel good — and, let's face it, she's probably already a little stressed. Very little upside can be gained, and huge potential downside. Keep it together and drive safely.

Chapter **7**

Lights, Camera, Action: Giving Birth

inally, the big moment is here — you and your partner have probably been thinking about the time when your baby is born for most of the pregnancy. The somewhat unpredictable nature of the onset of labour adds to the excitement. Going through labour is a bit like doing your first parachute jump — except that someone pushes you out the door whether you're ready or not. So enjoy the ride!

In this chapter, you find out about making it through labour. I also cover some medical stuff you might experience during labour and guide you to welcoming your baby to the world. Finally, I give you some useful information on how to get through the first few hours and days with your newborn baby.

Helping Your Partner through Childbirth

In Chapter 6, I ran through the three stages of labour, and the three phases within the first stage. In the following sections, I provide more detail on how you can get involved and support your partner at each stage and phase.

Offering support during the latent phase

Many women spend the *latent phase* of labour at home, where they're more comfortable and have lots of room to move around. Even if you're planning a hospital birth, staying at home for as long as is feasible is usually best. Some mums who go to the hospital too early tense up because they're at the hospital (which can slow down labour) and experience fatigue earlier than if they'd stayed at home for longer. Plus, it can get boring at the hospital if you're there half a day (or more) early.

Once in a hospital setting, the focus is fully on the labour. When you and your partner are at home, you can feel more relaxed and the emphasis isn't just on those contractions.

During this stage, especially if it's at night, focus on rest. Your partner can sleep between contractions or even through them — they'll wake her up if they start moving along. Relaxation really is the key to the dilation (opening) of the cervix (which is often why labour begins at night). Now is not the time for mum to feel like she needs to vacuum the house so everything's ready for her return. Depending on what time of day it is when labour begins, however, some activity is good, and an easy walk can stimulate contractions and help progress things if contractions are off to a sluggish start. The emphasis, though, is on ensuring you are both in a good space physically for when things move along later on. So whatever promotes calm and relaxation is best.

Contractions during the latent phase shouldn't be too unmanageable and you can try these techniques to relieve whatever discomfort your partner is feeling:

>> Apply a heatpack or hot water bottle to your partner's bump or lower back where she feels the most pain.

>> Give your partner a gentle back rub with some massage oil.

>> Run a bath or turn on the shower for your partner — warm water soothes, and a bath can soften the strength of the contractions. If her membranes have ruptured (that is, her waters have broken), a shower is the better option.

>> Keep your partner moving (as long as it's not the middle of the night). Movement can help labour progress and gravity

means the baby's weight puts pressure on the cervix, helping it to dilate.

» Turn down the lights.

» Offer drinks and snacks as needed.

REMEMBER

Your partner may not want food but having it on standby is always good. Offer it when you think she might be open to having something. Make her your focus — you may have to suggest she drinks something or show her the different foods at times when you think she may be hungry. She'll let you know very quickly what she needs or doesn't want.

Ramping up into active phase and then second stage

As contractions get stronger and you move into the active and transition phases and then the second stage of labour, you can continue with the pain relief techniques outlined in the preceding section. Let your partner guide you as to what she needs. At certain points, your partner won't have the ability to do anything other than ride out a contraction, especially in the second stage when she's putting everything into pushing the baby out. Holding up your partner's body and letting her lean on you in whatever way she needs is a great help to her during this demanding time.

REMEMBER

During the active phase of labour (when the cervix dilates from four to seven centimetres), contractions build for about 20 to 30 seconds. They peak for between 15 and 30 seconds and then they gradually come down as the uterus uses up the oxygen in the muscles and needs time to build that up again. After a total of around 60 seconds, that contraction is over. Some are slightly shorter. Some fizzle and do nothing. But most will be consistent.

TIP

To support your partner best during the contraction process, talk her through each contraction. Remind her that contractions are like a wave. Once the contraction is over, the focus is to rest, regroup and relax. Offer ice. Every 40 minutes, see if your partner needs to empty her bladder or to stand and walk. (This applies downwards pressure in a healthy way.) Watch and see if any areas need a strong rub or gentle massage. Reassure your partner that relaxation continues to be the key to dilation, and that riding the contractions instead of resisting them is how they work at their best.

As the birth gets closer, the body increases the contraction rate and intensity — particularly during transition (when the cervix dilates from seven to ten centimetres). It's almost time for the pushing to happen. Contractions build quickly and peak for longer with less time between them. Each contraction still lasts for about 60 seconds, but the build is only 10 seconds, the peak is 40 seconds, and the slowdown is shorter.

This is really an 'all hands on deck' time. You can ride that contraction wave with your partner by talking her through it. Reassure her that it's doing what it should. Encourage her to take a deep breath as it begins and to relax into it, knowing it's doing its job, and opening the cervix for the baby to come out. As you see the intensity start to ebb, confirm with her it's going. Reassure her everything is okay and happening as it should.

TIP

Between contractions, you might find your partner becoming anxious about the next contraction. This is where you remind her to use this 'down' time for what it's meant to be for her: a time to relax, breathe, rest and recover. Acknowledge that another contraction will come, and that you'll work together through it — and then it will go and the baby will be that much closer. But also acknowledge the current calm. Your coaching as contractions come and go like waves will keep you both present and focused, and will become an experience that binds you together powerfully.

Remembering it's not about you

Labour can take a long time. You may get a chance to have a breather between contractions, or you may not. Giving all your energy to your partner is exhausting, but this is not about you just now — and the exhaustion you're feeling is nothing compared to hers. Your partner needs you. She needs to know you are there, that you believe in her, and that she can rely on you to coach and guide her, gently, through this.

Perhaps you've heard stories of soon-to-be dads who watched a game of footy while their wife laboured. Or they closed a business deal, went to the pub for a drink with the boys, or did some other stuff that made for a 'great story' years later. But these kinds of actions (and stories) are neither cool nor manly. They are not what make your partner feel supported. I'll say it again: this process is not about you. Paradoxically, the more you make it about your partner and her comfort, the better the experience actually becomes for you — particularly when you look back on it years later.

BEING THE CALM IN THE EYE OF THE TRANSITION STORM

By the time transition arrives, your partner is often kaput. Labour is long and physically taxing. It often happens at night, so exhaustion can become overpowering. This is the time when you bring your very best you to the support-person role. During transition, your partner may cry. She may tell you she wants to give up and it's all too much. Or you might cop a barrage of verbal abuse like you've never heard before.

At this point, *you* may also wonder what's going on. You may feel help-less and *want* it to stop. You'll be hearing her say she can't do it any-more and you may question yourself about what right you have to encourage her to keep going. Can you do anything that will really help her? The answer is definite 'yes'. The greatest thing you can do when she is at her lowest is to become her strength when hers is failing. You are the one who can see the progress made when she's caught in the middle of the storm. You are the one who knows that each contrac-tion *will* end and huge progress is being made with each mountainous contraction.

You may feel like you have no right to say it, but tell her with intent and conviction:

- 'I'm here. You can do this. I believe in you.'
- 'Just get through this next one. I'm here with you — we can do this.'
- 'You'll have a break after this next contraction. Just relax — I'm so proud of you.'
- 'You're doing so well — you're almost there.'

Let her know you're there. Reassure her of how brave she is and that she'll be okay. The transition phase is when you see the unspeakable sacrifice a woman makes to bring a child into the world. If you're lucky, witnessing this will humble you in ways you didn't know were possible, and will make you love your partner to a depth you weren't aware existed. If you're man enough, this is the time you tell her all of that and more. And it's the moment you realise just how strong this woman you love actually is.

Acceptable things for dads to do during labour include

>> Crying (actually, sobbing) when the baby arrives and you see your partner as the most impossibly strong human on the planet

>> Doing some stretching exercises to keep fresh and fend off sleep

>> Drinking water or juices to keep yourself in good condition for the ride ahead

>> Eating snacks

>> Fainting

>> Getting some fresh air

>> Going to the toilet (as long as it's not too often and doesn't take too long)

>> Leaving the room because you're feeling unwell or faint (again, don't be away too long)

The following actions are really in stark contrast to the future super dad you're aiming to be:

>> Bringing your office work to do on your laptop

>> Inviting people (including family and friends) into the delivery suite

>> Joking with the staff instead of giving your partner your focus

>> Playing video games on your mobile

>> Sneaking into the vacant birthing suite next door to have a kip or snoring in a recliner in the birthing suite

>> Talking to others on the phone or in the room while your partner's contracting or needs you (which is most of the time)

>> Telling your partner how tired you are

>> Watching your favourite show or sport on your phone

Giving Nature a Helping Hand

Sometimes during labour, nature needs help to get your baby out into the world. Lots of reasons exist for this: the baby may be in distress, your partner's health is in jeopardy, or your partner's exhausted and wants the baby out now! None of the interventions covered in the following sections can really be anticipated. Keep in touch with your partner and, if she's adamant she doesn't want any intervention, be her advocate. But don't be the decision maker. It's her choice, not yours, and hospital staff (or the midwife if it's a home birth) will want to hear what she wants — not you. Talk together if you have time and options, and help her make the decision that is best for her and the baby. You can be the rational and kind part of the decision-making process.

REMEMBER

When the medical equipment comes out, try not to freak out. Some of it can look scarier than it really is. The equipment's going to help you meet your baby sooner rather than later.

Ventouse

A *ventouse* is a vacuum extractor that helps pull the baby out of the *birth canal*. A ventouse is used when the baby's head is low in the birth canal but needs an extra bit of oomph to help her along. The baby's heart rate may indicate she's in distress, or her position may be making it tricky for her to be born naturally.

A suction cup is put onto the baby's head and your partner may have to have an *episiotomy*, which is a cut to the vaginal opening, to make room for the cup to go in. A ventouse can cause swelling to the top of the baby's head, but usually causes little or no trauma to the mother and baby. Episiotomies are easily stitched up by competent doctors and, while your partner will be tender for a while, won't have any impact on long-term comfort (or your sex life) going forward. Don't get involved here. Let the medical professionals do their thing and trust that it will be okay.

Forceps

Forceps look like a scary pair of tongs. They are used to grip the baby's head on both sides and pull her out of the birth canal. Forceps aren't used as often as ventouse these days because of the risk that the mother's insides (including her pelvic floor muscles) can be damaged, not to mention the bruising and risk of damage to the baby's head. An episiotomy is routinely required with forceps use as well.

Emergency caesarean

The big daddy of medical interventions during labour is the emergency caesarean. These kinds of caesareans are called 'emergency' to distinguish them from elective caesareans, where you opt for birth this way. All caesareans take place in an operating theatre, and you have to wear a gown and cover your hair. Your partner is given an *epidural* to numb pain (although, in some cases, the caesarean has to be performed under general anaesthetic), and an incision is made in your partner's belly, usually near the pubic bone, known as a bikini cut. The abdominal muscles are parted and the *peritoneal* cavity is opened to make way for the uterus. The uterus is then opened, and the baby and placenta are brought out.

Having a caesarean isn't an 'easy' way of having a baby; the procedure is major surgery, and you may not want to look behind the sheet that stops your partner from seeing her insides come out. (Partners are rarely allowed in the room anyhow.) Having a caesarean also means your partner takes weeks to recover, and she isn't able to drive or lift anything heavy for up to six weeks. She's also on pain medication and has to rest a lot as she recovers, and stays in hospital for four or five days.

If your partner had her heart set on a vaginal birth, or a natural drug-free birth, and the birth hasn't worked out that way, she may be feeling disappointed and upset with herself. Add this to the hormones rampaging through her body and you have one sad little mummy. Give her all the love and support you can muster right now — she needs you.

The Big Moment's Arrived

The moment your child is born is a peak experience that's difficult to describe — unique, beautiful and out of this world. Enjoy it. You may find yourself shedding a tear or two at this important moment. In fact, you could find yourself a sobbing mess. Cherish this snapshot in time because the moment you clap eyes on your child for the first time can't be rehearsed or repeated.

Cutting the cord

After the placenta is born and your baby is coping on her own without help from mum, the umbilical cord is clamped and set up to cut. This small task can take on several significant meanings for your new family. For your partner, cutting the cord can represent the end of her pregnancy and the start of motherhood. For you, the process might symbolise your part in your new family. Most importantly for your little one, cutting the cord symbolises a point in time where all life support systems from mum are cut off and her body has to sustain her. Cutting the cord is a big deal, so embrace the significance and enjoy the procedure.

REMEMBER

Not every dad wants to cut the cord or sees it in the ceremonial way I've just described it. Some dads are uncomfortable with anything medical, don't like the blood, or perhaps they see cutting the cord as the cutting of the literal tie that bonds mum to bub. It's not a requirement, and if you don't see it as your thing — or you're too overwhelmed and involved in comforting your partner and staring at your baby — don't feel like you need to do it. Of all the things you can be involved in during the birth process, this one is not going to be the thing you remember most.

TIP

The cord is really rather thick and gnarly, so apply some elbow grease and give it a good strong cut. If the cord-cutting is a ceremonial aspect that means a lot to you, perhaps ask your midwife or other support person to take a photo.

When time stops — meeting your baby

So you're looking at your child for the first time. The experience can be incredible, scary, bewildering and amazing, all in the space of a few seconds. Time seems to stop as you feel all these emotions washing over you.

Take a moment now to have a good look at what's been cooking for nine months — little fingers, little toes — because mum may have her hands full being taken care of by medical staff right now.

Notice all her little features and enjoy the amazing sight of a newborn baby. Typically, you aren't rushed anymore once your baby has been checked and is handed to you. So you can easily take some time out to make your first acquaintance with the little one. What a great start to a lifelong bond. As dad, you're probably eager to hold that baby close. But usually mum gets first dibs for skin-on-skin time. This is important for mum and bub, and not interfering with that time is best. You get plenty of opportunity soon enough.

Keeping your cool

It's been a long day (or two). You've let your partner and your midwife or doctor guide you through the process and you have to admit to yourself you've been a pretty damn awesome support crew. You've advocated for your partner, you've kept her well stocked with food and drink, massaged till you thought your arms would fall off, and she's right now looking forward to a cuddle with your baby and a good rest. But you may find the demands of the system — the midwife needs to zip off to another appointment before you're ready, or you can't be transferred from the delivery suite to the ward because of paperwork — overrides you right now, so keep advocating for your partner and child if they need it.

Welcoming Your Baby to the Real World

Once bub has finally arrived, thinking that the hard yards are over may be tempting. You may be gazing blissfully at your new baby, enjoying video calls with family, or may be tempted to dash home for a couple of hours' sleep. Cool it for a few minutes more because you have more stuff to get through yet.

What happens immediately after birth

Making sure your new baby is in good health is top priority. Most likely, your baby has come out a rather scary shade of blue or grey, but within a few minutes of breathing actual air, she starts to take on a rosier complexion. She's covered in vernix, the waxy coating that protected her skin in the womb. Your baby may even have a pointy head, caused by her soft baby skull plates moving as she came down the birth canal. Yes, babies can be a bit of a sight when they first emerge into the world! Some babies howl the house down when they're born. Others just like to take things a bit more quietly and have a look around first.

If your baby needs a bit of help breathing, your carer may massage her back with a warm cloth, or suction fluid from her mouth or nose. Don't worry, she'll be good as gold soon.

At one minute and five minutes after birth, your carer does an Apgar test on your little one, giving her an *Apgar score* on a scale of one to ten, with one being lowest and ten being highest. (It's called an Apgar test in honour of the doctor who invented it, and saved millions of babies lives as a result.) Your newborn has five criteria to jump through: colour, pulse rate, reflexes, muscle tone and breathing. This test alerts your carer to any concerns about the baby's health.

After — and perhaps even before — her first test, your carer dries your baby and hands her over to mum for some skin-on-skin time before anything else. (Baby may be placed straight onto your partner's abdomen with a blanket covering while the test is performed and then moved up to her chest.) This skin-to-skin contact is super-important so, tempting as it may be to try to hold your little one right away, leave her lying on mum's chest for as long as you can. This is their time to bond. Yours will come later. You have a whole life to live with this baby. But right now, let mum hold that little one and soak it in. Be in the moment and make it theirs, not yours. (And grab a photo or two. These moments are precious.)

If you and your partner have discussed dad also having skin on skin contact with bub, wait patiently and, once mum has had her time, you can have yours. Let the carers know this is something you have both discussed when the timing is right. Then close your eyes, hold that baby close, and soak it all in.

While all of this is going on your carer measures your baby's length and head circumference and weighs your baby. Ideally, they do this sensitively while allowing for that skin-to-skin time for mum and your little one. Those details go into your child's personal health book. Some practitioners in some states take a footprint as well. Check with your carer if you would like one to keep.

While bub is having a snuggle with mum (or dad if mum's too knackered), your carer puts a plastic band around her ankle with your names, date of birth and weight. These can become mementos of your baby's birth when they come off a few days later.

The first few hours

Once all the commotion has died down, a few practical matters must be attended to. Have you started ringing friends and family yet? Sending a photo to your social feed/timeline with the time, date and basic info is always a quick and easy way to get the message out to family and friends. (Get your partner's approval before you post it though!) Making a quick call or have a video chat with closest family is also good form — they prefer a direct call to finding out on social media, and they've normally been anxiously waiting for this moment.

Meanwhile, mum and bub usually have their skin-on-skin time and start to get to know each other a bit, and then bub has some food. Yep — feeding your baby is going to be mum's number one priority for some time, so they may as well get stuck into the process now. Your carer helps mum and bub get comfy with a first breastfeed or, if bottle feeding is a necessity, helps with the mechanics of getting your little one taking her bottle.

Once that's all taken care of, getting bub dressed and getting mum into a nice warm shower are next on the agenda. Your partner is likely to be pretty well done by now, so you may need to give her a hand standing up and getting about, or you may have a chance to get to know your baby a bit better while your partner's busy. Skin-to-skin contact between you and your baby might be best to happen now.

REMEMBER

Baby needs to be kept warm because they are moist and body temperature can lower. Keep your baby close during skin-to-skin time. Your warm hands will also help or the hospital may have a baby blanket to drape around bub, depending on the protocols.

TIP

A bit of food and drink wouldn't go amiss now, either. A long time has passed since either of you had a decent meal. Taking care of any food cravings your partner couldn't eat while being pregnant is also high on the agenda. That said, all you may feel like is some well-deserved rest. If you're in a hospital, see to it that any formalities are dealt with quickly so you, your partner and your brand new little one can enjoy some quiet recovery time.

The first few days

Many parents can be lulled into thinking their baby is an angel in the first 24 hours. Babies can be very sleepy and settled for the first day, and you may be fooled! But this period is also a very busy time, getting feeding established and finding your feet in your new role as dad. Your baby should be having about six feeds in a 24-hour period to start off with, so supporting mum by taking care of nappy changes, burping or anything else that needs attending to can help her out a lot. If mum is still in hospital, you can be a real hero dad for spending as much time as possible with the baby so mum can rest some more.

Meconium

Your perfect, cute little bundle produces the foulest, stickiest, goopiest poo imaginable in the first few days of life. This black tar is called *meconium* and it's perfectly normal. Meconium is nature's way of flushing out all the various fluids and contents of your baby's intestines. The meconium is gone within a few days. After that, if fully breastfed, your baby's poo should turn to a strange orangey-yellow colour. The great news is a newborn's poo hardly smells, easing you gently into the changing soiled nappies routine.

Going home

If your baby was born in hospital, your carer and the hospital decide when your partner and baby can go home. For some new mums, going home can't come fast enough — and if everyone is healthy and everything is in order, discharge can be arranged within about four hours of birth! Other mums may feel they need longer in hospital for the support a 24-hour, on-call midwife brings, or they might not feel physically up to leaving hospital, depending on how the birth went. Don't let the hospital push you out if you're not ready for it. But if your partner feels like home would be more comfortable, get the all-clear and go for it. If you have any concerns, talk them over with your carer — but keep in mind that you can't stay in the relative safety of the hospital forever!

Blues

About day three after birth, mum may feel a bit low. This is perfectly normal and does pass. Your partner may burst into tears for no reason (that she can tell you, anyway) or just feel overwhelmed by responsibility. Chances are, your partner is also sore in all sorts of places, and performing simple personal hygiene tasks or even just going to the toilet can be really tricky. Do your dad thing and try to support your partner by helping out, telling her she's awesome and enjoying your baby. Know that this will usually pass as her hormone levels adjust. Be kind and helpful, and be glad it's not your body going through all those huge changes.

The initial post-birth blues have nothing to do with postnatal depression, which is likely to come later if you or your partner end up experiencing it. See Chapter 10 for more on postnatal depression.

4

Life After Birth

Find out everything you need to know about baby care, routines and your baby's every need — when your baby is completely vulnerable and dependent on you for everything in his life.

Understand the key health risks your baby is exposed to during the first few weeks and months, and how to maintain a healthy home.

Learn about the help and support organisations you can rely on during your fatherhood journey.

Chapter **8**
The First Few Days and Weeks

Your baby is finally here. Does being a dad feel 'real' now? If not, don't worry. The first few days and weeks after birth can feel surreal. For some dads, having a child feels life-changing. For others, it's almost like the birth happened and now life resumes. Work commitments pile up. The world keeps spinning. Whether it's an earth-shattering change or life-as-normal, becoming a dad will create changes for you, and if it's been 'no biggie' so far, you can rest assured that the times, they are a-changing.

If you felt a bit left out during pregnancy and birth, now is your time to get stuck in. Your baby is here and needs time with dad as often as possible. Realising that your baby is an actual person and that you're responsible for him now can also be quite daunting for some new dads. (At the other end of the continuum, some dads take it all in their stride.)

In this chapter, I give you some shortcuts on your journey to being a great dad with guides to the practical aspects of baby care, such as changing nappies, and dressing and bathing your baby.

You get the lowdown on feeding, sleeping, burping and dealing with crying. I also talk about how having a baby shakes things up in your life like nothing else can, and look at ways to cope with that change.

Dealing With the Aftershock

Starting out with your new baby — a vulnerable, unfathomable being — can be a scary experience. Placing the baby into the car and driving home from hospital may be the first time you've been nervous behind the wheel of the car for a long time. Stepping through the door with your little bundle as you come home from the hospital, or waving goodbye to the midwife if your baby was born at home, are momentous steps on the path to becoming a family. You may feel a little daunted flying solo with your partner and the new baby, but that's quite normal. Every parent in the world has probably felt the same. Don't stress and simply take each day as it comes.

It's life but not as you know it

Remember last week when you slept in on Sunday, had a leisurely brunch with your partner and then went for a walk taking just the house keys and some money to stop off at the shop on the way home? You're going to be able to do that again, but not for many years. Getting your head around how life works now can be a struggle, but that's where dads can shine once more. As dads, we're great at adapting quickly to new situations and making the best out of any challenge we face (say 'YES!').

Looking after a newborn is literally a 24-hour, seven-day-a-week job and is exhausting. Expect your baby to sleep a lot in the first couple of days, but he needs a feed every two to four hours, so even at night he wakes up. Even if mum is breastfeeding, you don't get off night duty. You can help by doing any nappy changes and burping so mum doesn't feel she's doing everything. If you're bottle feeding, you can take turns so at least one of you gets a decent stretch of rest.

You may already be tired from supporting your partner after a long labour and birth and, because your baby is waking every few hours, you're not getting a good eight hours sleep like you used to. You can't catch up on the sleep you've missed, but you can minimise your own exhaustion by resting when the baby sleeps. This goes for both you and your partner in these heady first days. Getting used to the idea of taking turns for everything is worthwhile. While one of you is busy, the other should rest or catch up on some much needed sleep. Here's a perfect opportunity to shine as a dad by sharing the load with mum.

REMEMBER

Apart from breastfeeding, dads can do everything around a baby and no natural disadvantage or disposition exists. You're just as qualified at handling a newborn as mum. In other words, you both don't know much and are learning as you go.

Any information you've read about caring for babies tells you lots of chores have to be done in the first weeks. That's not necessarily true. On days where everything goes smoothly — baby wakes, has a feed, is burped, gurgles cutely for a bit and then goes down for a nap without a whimper — you may wonder what all the fuss was about and sit around twiddling your thumbs. But not every day goes smoothly. And not every cycle of feeding, burping and sleeping goes smoothly in a day. At any point, the following may happen:

>> Bub's nappy overflows or leaks.

>> Your baby shows symptoms you decide to have checked by a midwife or doctor.

>> Your baby spills (vomits) — called *posseting* — after a feed.

Events such as those just listed mean you suddenly have to deal with something unexpected and your plan for the day is disrupted. Get used to disruption because it happens a lot with children. Life becomes a lot less predictable and plans go awry. But you can see this unpredictability as a good thing, and you can enjoy it rather than choose to be a victim of it. Expect to have to change your baby's clothes (and yours) frequently, clean the carpet or furniture, or visit the after-hours clinic. Your baby also may have days where he just refuses to sleep or cries incessantly — which is a special kind of torture — and you can end up spending an entire day or night rocking him, walking him in a stroller or carrying him in a sling just to get some peace. If you can count on one thing with newborns, it's to expect the unexpected.

Take offers of help whenever you can. Having a person close to you whom you can call when things are trying and understands you're running on empty is very handy. You could ask friends to drop over a meal for the two of you, take over pushing the stroller while you sit in the backyard away from the crying, or hang out the washing. A few hours break from the baby can make all the difference.

If you feel you're at the end of your tether, don't despair. Get someone to give you a break for a couple of hours and chances are you feel much better.

At home with your newborn baby

Falling into the trap of letting mum take care of everything to do with the baby can be easy. Some mums have a tendency to 'take over' and secretly or unconsciously harbour the belief that dads are somewhat inadequate when it comes to dealing with babies. Of course, this is not so. No competition is taking place to see who's better at looking after bub. In some cases, you may have to tell mum to go away and do something else while you look after the baby.

Take care of bub early on so you become more and more confident at handling your baby. You can consider yourself 'graduated' from dad school when you are perfectly happy to spend an entire day alone with bub (although that may be a while down the track if mum is breastfeeding).

If you develop a mindset of seeing your baby as a developing person who needs your help every step of the way, rather than a source of work and chores, you're already onto a winner in becoming a future super dad. If you've decided to adhere to a strict routine, or the baby is unsettled or unwell, seeing him as a problem that needs to be fixed, or a timetable that needs to be met, can be tempting. He may seem like a blob that just eats, poos and sleeps, but a lot's going on inside that little baby right now. Although he can't show you quite yet, he's getting to know you.

Hierarchies at home

In the first months of life, your baby is going to develop a special kind of 'attachment relationship' with the people he is most involved with (usually you, mum, and perhaps a grandparent).

That attachment simply represents the quality of the connection your baby shares with people around him. Here's the thing that can be hard to take for every new dad: no matter how much you try, in most circumstances an attachment hierarchy is going to develop, and you'll probably be number two on that hierarchy, and maybe even number three. But — and this is the critical aspect — the more time you spend engaging with your little one, the more comfortable he becomes with you caring for him, even in the absence of mum (who really needs a break now and then).

In the early weeks, your newborn stares at you, sussing out your face, learning the sound of your voice and snuggling into you for snoozes. These are important bonding times. Attachment relationships are being established. Mum bonds in a way we can't (if breastfeeding), and mum also has a 40-week head start on this relationship thanks to pregnancy! But do this stuff well and your baby will be smiling up at you in no time.

Babies don't usually smile with intention and control until six weeks — although they can appear to be smiling (grandma will tell you it's just wind), which is nice even if it is uncontrolled. You know when the smile is intentional. He looks you in the eye and his face lights up like you're the best thing he's ever seen (which, of course, you are). At that point, you just melt inside and you may think that being a dad is the coolest thing you've ever experienced. And it confirms that you're definitely on that attachment hierarchy.

When your baby holds your gaze and checks you out in detail, a lot of developmental work is happening in his brain. Give him every opportunity to look at you. Breastfeeding mums have the advantage that this happens naturally during feeds, so you need to carve out some extra time with bub to get your fair share of baby time. Your baby's eyesight is quite limited in the early weeks and months. They see best things that are around 20 centimetres away — which, cleverly, is about the distance from mum's boob to her face. That's the distance the builds bonds in the early days.

Be a 100 per cent dad. Do the full spectrum of care tasks — changing your baby's nappies, bathing him and wiping spew off your shoulder — in the first few days because that's how your baby bonds with you. Performing these tasks tends to give you a different perspective on life and, after a while, you might find that little dramas like baby poo on the carpet are really no big deal.

YOUNG DADS

Being a father, no matter the age you become one, is about commitment; commitment to being there for a new young life, and guiding that new person towards adulthood and independence. For young men who find themselves becoming fathers, the commitment is no different — although, without the advantages of age and maturity, fatherhood can be even more of a challenge.

In addition, your relationship with the mother may not be a stable one, your parents may think you're too young and, therefore, not prepared to be a father, and tension may exist between your family and the mother's. Some people may think not having the baby at all is the better option.

But the more you show you're committed, the more people respect your determination, and the more your baby feels the love and security having a father brings. You can show your commitment by being involved with your baby from the day you find out your partner is pregnant. Go to pregnancy check-ups and antenatal classes, start making arrangements for how you're going to financially support your partner and child, and show that you're man enough for this very important job. Enlist the support of both your and your partner's families.

To be legally recognised as the baby's father, you need to have your name on the child's birth certificate. Doing so makes having access to your child easier if your relationship with his mother breaks down.

For resources for young dads, take a look at MensLine Australia (mensline.org.au/being-a-dad). The service also provides professional counsellors who can provide information and support for all father and parenting issues. You can call them on 1300 78 99 78.

You've got the blues

Expect mum to shed some tears in the first week. Hormones are playing war games in her body right now and she's likely to be up and down like a yo-yo. Sometimes the best you can do is to listen, remain calm even if she has a go at you and stay positive at all times. These are just clouds passing and chances are her mood changes in a few hours. So don't sweat the small quarrels, emotional outbursts or little annoyances.

What you may not know is that dads can get the blues after birth, too. At these times, communicating well with your partner about what you're going through is really important.

Sometimes the blues can morph into postnatal depression (PND), a serious mental health issue for new parents. Have a look at Chapter 10 for more about PND.

Looking After a Newborn

So now that you've got the baby, what do you do with her? How do you look after her? Feeling responsible for a new person can be hugely overwhelming, but babies are pretty straightforward. All they really need is love, food, warmth, sleep and a clean pair of undies.

In general, newborns exist in a 24-hour cycle of sleeping, feeding, being awake and sleeping again. Your baby tires very easily and is awake for only about an hour or so at a time. A large chunk of that time she's being fed, burped and changed if necessary, but time is available for a bit of interaction with dad, like story time (tell her anything you want — she loves to hear your voice), a few songs or even a walk outside together before the next nap time.

REMEMBER

Depending on where you live, your midwife or carer visits you or you visit her in the first few days and weeks after the birth to monitor your baby's growth and your partner's wellbeing, and to see how you're getting on in your new lives as a family. You then pass into the care of your child health nurse. So, if you ever feel you don't know where to turn or who to turn to, your carer, midwife or child health nurse should be your first port of call. You have regular appointments to visit your child health nurse as your child grows, and in some cases they can come and see you. The hospital where your partner gave birth may also have day clinics where you can take your little one if you're having problems in a particular area, such as sleeping or feeding.

TIP

Help from a registered nurse is available at all hours of the day and night through healthdirect on 1800 022 222. Most states also run a nurse-on-call service, so check with your carer what's available, and have the numbers saved in your phone.

Getting your hands dirty

In your dad role, you get to master a few practical jobs that are probably entirely new to you — until now.

Nappy changing 101

No magic is involved in changing a nappy; they're actually really easy (see Figure 8-1). Being prepared before you start is the key, as is keeping cool when the nappy you're taking off is fuller than you thought it may be. To change a nappy, you need

>> A change table or change mat on the floor, bed or sofa where you have lots of space around you and good access to your baby lying in front of you

>> A clean nappy, changing mat and barrier cream or powder

>> A nappy bag (small plastic bag) to put the soiled nappy in

>> Baby wipes or a bowl of warm water and some cotton wool or cloth standing by to wash down bub's bum

>> Towels or extra cloth nappies within reach just in case a last-minute explosion or leak occurs while his nappy is off

FIGURE 8-1: How to change a nappy.

REMEMBER

To minimise the risk of your baby falling from the bed or change table while you change him, either keep a hand on him at all times, or change him on a mat on the floor.

Complaining about how bad bub's nappy stinks doesn't win you any extra points with your partner. Keep it together, get the job done without complaint, and watch the way she admires you for your willingness to step up to the plate.

TIP

If you're a gadget dad, you may want to check out baby wipe warmers. Often baby wipes can feel really cold to a baby so these devices help to warm the wipes.

As I talk about in Chapter 7, your baby's first poos are called meconium and they're unforgettable — sticky, greenish-black and tar-like. Your baby's poos gradually change colour as his digestive system is cleaned out and he adjusts to his new food

The colour of your baby's poo depends on the type of food:

» Breastfed baby poos are runnier than meconium, and are an orange-yellow colour.

» Formula-fed baby poos are firmer and a green-mustard colour — and most people agree that they stink more.

If you're reading this before you've had your baby, talking about the colour and consistency of baby poo may seem very odd. But you may find poo discussions become part of your new social chitchat with your partner and other parents.

REMEMBER

To help prevent nappy rash, give your baby some nappy-free time each day. Allow the skin to be exposed to the air and light. Use a barrier cream or powder when he has a nappy on to protect his skin.

Bathing

Babies don't need baths every day, but a regular clean around their bottoms to prevent nappy rash, and around the face and neck where dribbled and regurgitated milk can collect, is a good idea. Some babies don't like to be naked for long; others love being in the water.

REMEMBER

For babies who aren't fond of a bath yet, 'topping and tailing' is an option. This practice is when you wipe baby's face, neck, hands and bottom with damp cotton wool or a soft cloth instead of giving them a full bath.

ELIMINATION COMMUNICATION

The practice of elimination communication (EC), also known as infant potty training or natural infant hygiene, means dispensing with nappies and reading your baby's cues telling you when he needs to relieve himself. You simply learn when junior needs to go and pop him on the potty. Using sounds like 'ssss' and getting him used to specific places where he can 'go potty' can also act as cues that trigger your child to relieve himself.

Those who practise EC say the method empowers children by letting them take charge of their own toileting, encourages a stronger bond between parent and child as you learn to understand your child's needs and cues better, and makes your baby feel more secure because he knows you're going to take care of him when he needs you to.

Practising EC doesn't mean you have to go the whole hog and be nappy-free completely — many parents try EC only when they're outdoors, or only during the day. Others encourage potty use at set times of the day, such as right after waking up or before or after a bath. If you're interested in giving EC a go, take your time and see what works for you. Being watchful and conscious of your child's cues is the first place you need to start. Be prepared with a potty and some old cloth nappies to take care of accidents.

Take a look at www.nappyfree.com.au for more information.

Holding your newborn securely at all times when you're bathing him is important. The best way is to place your arm under the shoulders so that your forearm is supporting his head and your hand is holding the shoulder and upper arm furthest away from you. Hold on securely — he can be a wriggly little monster even at this young age.

Here are some tips for bathing your little one:

>> Check the temperature of the bath with both hands (immerse them to a point above the wrists) and be sure to agitate the water to remove any hot spots. The water should be lukewarm — that is, if the water feels hot, it's too hot; if it feels cold, it's too cold. You can also check the temperature with a bath thermometer.

>> Ensure the room temperature is quite warm. Your baby is naked and wet, so he can feel quite cold even when you feel perfectly fine in your clothes, especially when his head is wet for extended periods (try washing the head last).

>> Collect everything you need before you start — including a cloth or cotton wool and a towel. Bub shouldn't need soap, shampoo or cleanser yet; let the natural oils in his skin do the work.

>> Gunk can collect in all those rolls he's sporting on his legs and arms, so give them a wipe. The same goes for your baby's hands, so unfurl those little fists to wipe his palms.

Pay particular attention to the neck. Spilt milk rolls down the neck and can sneak into that chubby triple chin he's got at the moment.

>> Wash his face, hair and neck where milk often collects with a soft cloth or cotton wool.

>> When cleaning baby girls' bottoms, wipe from front to back.

You don't need to pull back your little boy's foreskin to wash underneath.

>> When wiping your baby's face, wipe his eyes from inner to outer using cooled boiled water and cotton wool. This helps prevent an eye infection. If he has a sticky eye, as is common in the first weeks after birth, you can also use this technique. You may want to do this before giving him a full bath, while he's still got his clothes on.

TIP

Take a phone with you when you bathe your baby. Sometimes you may find you've forgotten something or need help, but you should never leave a baby unattended in the bath. Not even for 5 or 10 seconds. (Babies can drown in a few centimetres of water.) A phone is really handy if have forgotten something and your partner or another person is elsewhere in the house.

TIP

Your baby sports a little stump of *umbilical cord* for about five to ten days after birth. The stump is kind of shrivelled and not that appealing to look at, but it needs to be kept dry and clean to prevent infection. All you have to do is wash it with cotton wool and warm water when bathing baby or changing his nappy and pat it dry. Fold down the front of his nappy to stop the nappy rubbing against the cord and irritating it. If in doubt about the cord, call your midwife or doctor.

Dressing

Newborns aren't big fans of getting dressed and undressed, so keep clothing simple. Sleepsuits with domes or a zip down the front are perfect for these early days when bub is in and out of bed or having his nappy changed a lot during the day.

In general, your baby should be wearing one more thin layer than you. If you're not sure how hot or cold your baby is, put a finger down the back of his neck. He needs to feel warm rather than too hot or cold.

TIP

If your newborn seems irritated by something, the source of irritation can be as simple as a scratchy label rubbing his neck or a thread wrapping itself round his toe. Cutting off labels, especially if they feel rough or scratchy, is a good idea — but be sure to get the whole thing. That little edge can be a big irritant.

Feeding

Feeding your baby to help him grow and be healthy is an absolute given. But how do you feed him and when?

Breast or formula?

The World Health Organization recommends breastfeeding as the best way to provide nutrition for a baby. Breastmilk's the ideal food for your baby for at least the first six months of his life, providing targeted nutrition for his age and boosting his immunity. Breastmilk's always at the right temperature and generally readily available. Breastfeeding encourages bonding between mother and baby and can help with mum's health too. Last but not least, breastmilk's free. (For more on the benefits of breastfeeding for mum and bub, see Chapter 9.)

However, this isn't an ideal world and sometimes the situation just doesn't allow breastfeeding to work. Breastfeeding may not work for your family for many reasons. That's okay — an alternative to breastfeeding is available. Formula is a milk powder with added vitamins and nutrients to support growth and development, and plenty of babies thrive on it.

FEEDING IS ALL A MATTER OF STYLE

When you feed your baby can be just as controversial as *what* you feed your baby. Many experts and organisations such as the Australian Breastfeeding Association advocate *demand feeding*, which is letting the baby determine when he is fed rather than feeding him to a schedule. This often works best for most new parents. However, demand feeding may not work for your situation and feeding your baby at specific times may work best for you. A wide range of books is available with feeding plans to match your baby's age.

These books are controversial and most feeding experts recommend a more child-centred approach, but not every family can do that. An exhausted or depressed mum, or one with twins or triplets, are two examples of where a more structured approach might be needed.

Whatever you and your partner decide to feed your baby, pros to both breastfeeding and formula exist. In some cases, both breast-milk and formula can be fed to your baby, which means dads get more time in the feeding seat. Breastfeeding mums can also express milk using a breast pump, which means you can help with the feeding even if a can of formula is nowhere to be seen.

REMEMBER

As a dad, you can get out your advocating shoes again and support your partner in whichever method of feeding she needs or prefers. If your partner's given breastfeeding her best shot but it hasn't worked out, the situation can be tough emotionally for her. Your partner may feel like a failure, or less like a 'real' mother to her child. She may be sensitive to the opinions of others around her, family and health professionals included, who don't understand the decision. Don't worry about the opinions of others; you don't have to justify yourself to anyone. Be confident that you're doing the best for your family.

TIP

Before deciding what and how to feed your baby, get as much information as you can so you're fully informed of the choices and their implications.

Bottle feeding

If you're bottle feeding, you need the following gear:

>> Bottles and teats

>> Something to clean the bottles and teats in, such as a bottle steriliser unit for use in the microwave, a large bowl and sanitiser tablets, or a large pot that you can boil everything in, and a bottle brush

Formula should be made up right before a feed according to the instructions on the tin or packet. Have a supply of bottles and teats ready to go for when your baby's next feeling peckish to save you mucking about.

TIP

Even if your partner's breastfeeding, getting the bottle feeding equipment anyway is a good idea. Your partner may wish to express breastmilk, so you need the equipment included in the preceding list for bottle feeding. Bottles and feeding equipment used with breastmilk need to be sterilised and cleaned just as thoroughly as feeding equipment used for formula.

REMEMBER

Feeding your baby is about creating a nurturing relationship between you and your child, as well as food. Your baby is held close when being breastfed and the same should go for bottle feeding. You can hold your baby in the same loving way as if he were breastfed, sing to him or have a little chat while he feeds. You find he gazes up at you adoringly and checks out every little nook of your face.

How much and when?

Newborn babies love to eat. They grow rapidly and their stomachs are small, so they need regular feeds to keep them tanked up. Having regular feeds also encourages milk production. If your partner is breastfeeding, her milk supply adjusts to meet baby's demand.

Your baby tells you when he's hungry by:

>> Opening his mouth and thrusting his head to the side, as if rooting around to find your partner's breast.

>> Sucking his fists or clothing.

>> Crying, which is a late sign of hunger and means feed me now or else!

A good sign that you're on the right track with feeding your baby is that he's putting on about the right amount of weight for his age. Babies usually lose weight in the first two weeks after birth. After the first few weeks, bub generally gains around 200 to 300 grams per week. Don't worry — this rate slows as he gets older.

REMEMBER

Newborns usually need to be fed every two to three hours, or about eight to ten times in a 24-hour period. You know your baby is getting enough to eat because he has at least six to eight wet nappies per day, his wee is light yellow, not dark, and his poos are soft. If you're concerned, telephone your child health nurse, midwife or doctor.

Burping

Bringing up a good hearty belch may come naturally to you, but for bub, who can't sit up or stand and whose digestive system is still immature, a bit of air caught in his tummy or gut needs help to come out or it can be very painful. Usually a gentle pat on the back or a gentle rub anticlockwise (again on the back) does the trick. Your demure little prince comes out with a burp to make you proud.

You can use three good positions to burp your baby (see Figure 8-2):

>> Lying on your lap, with bub facing down

>> Sitting on your thigh, facing out

>> Over the shoulder, with bub's head held upright on your shoulder

Don't forget to support bub's wobbly head. To protect yourself against any posseting (white milky spew), drape a flat cloth nappy or muslin cloth over your shoulder or lap.

And, finally, if you haven't been pooed, peed or vomited on yet, you're not trying hard enough! Man up and get stuck in with the baby care tasks.

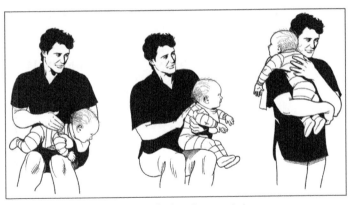

FIGURE 8-2: Three good positions for burping your baby.

TIP

If your baby is difficult to burp or seems uncomfortable, try getting him upright and moving around a bit. Putting him into a baby carrier and taking him for a walk (gently bouncing your baby with each step) can help all the trapped air escape and smooth the digestive process — and can be a great baby and dad bonding time.

Sleeping — you and the baby

Newborns wake regularly in the night and day for food, so getting a good eight-hour stretch of sleep is unlikely at this stage. As he gets older, your baby sleeps for longer chunks at night and stays awake for longer in the day.

Your baby tells you he's tired by

>> Grizzling

>> Making jerky, tense movements

>> Rubbing his eyes

>> Staring into space

>> Yawning

Crying is a late sign of tiredness and may mean your baby is overtired. When bub is overtired, he may be more difficult to settle because he's wound up about being tired.

Teaching your baby about night and day

Babies don't have a sense of day and night when they're born, so part of your role as dad is to teach them the difference. Babies usually follow a cycle of sleeping, feeding, burping, changing, playing and sleeping again during the day, but you can leave out the playing at night. Where you're animated and chatty in the day, you're all business at night, keeping the room dimly lit for feeds and nappy changes, and putting baby straight back to bed when you're done.

Having a bedtime routine can help signal that night is on the way and that's the time for sleeping.

Settling your baby

As many approaches to getting bub to sleep are available as there are children! How you get your baby to sleep is perhaps the most controversial topic. Strategies range from the *cry-it- out* approach, where you put your baby down for a sleep in a bassinet or cot and offer limited comfort to his cries until he falls asleep, to the *attachment parenting* philosophy of keeping bub in close contact with a parent in a sling or pouch to sleep and having him sleep in bed with you at night.

Other parents use a technique called *controlled crying*, where baby is left to cry for a short period of time — say, a couple of minutes — before being soothed and comforted, and then left for a slightly longer period. The length of time between visits is stretched out and eventually baby goes to sleep.

WARNING

Methods such as cry-it-out or controlled crying should not be attempted before baby is six months or older.

Some parenting experts warn against rocking your baby to sleep or doing anything where he falls asleep as a result of parent inter-vention, because bub becomes dependent on that technique to sleep. Putting your baby down sleepy but awake and letting him fall asleep on his own teaches him good sleep habits.

REMEMBER

The baby-sleep challenge is literally one of the hardest things you will navigate as a new dad. It creates a level of stress that is previ-ously unimaginable. Be aware that no-one is at their best when they're tired, so working out a way through this becomes a high priority early on.

Being never-endingly responsive to every whimper is ultimately unhelpful to your little one's sleep challenges, because it exhausts you and leaves you less able to be a great dad (and same goes for mum). But it can be distressing for everyone involved when the baby is screaming, it's late, and everyone is bone tired. Leaving the baby to cry it out is a heartbreaking approach for most parents, and doesn't seem to do much good for the bub. Plenty of ink has been spilt as people have debated how to deal with this challenge, so let's keep it simple here.

When your baby is whimpering, you can probably wait a few minutes and see whether he settles or becomes more upset. If your baby starts crying, you might want to briefly wait to see if things escalate. Sometimes stepping quietly into the room and giving him a pat or a short cuddle is all it takes. If your little one escalates things, check the nappy, see if he's hungry, try burping, and spend more time soothing. And remember that every child eventually sleeps through the night. It will pass.

TIP

Reach agreement with your partner before deciding which settling technique, method or routine to follow, because using different approaches tends not to work. Consistency is key.

REMEMBER

If you're having severe trouble settling your baby for days or weeks on end, call your midwife, child health nurse or community health care organisation. Sleep schools are also available throughout Australia, where a specially trained nurse guides you through the process of training your baby to sleep. A range of different programs are usually available for parents to attend, from two-night intensives, to five- or seven-night stays. These schools usually promote approaches that aren't consistent with more 'gentle' or 'attachment' parenting, so go in with your eyes open.

Swaddling

One technique for helping babies to sleep is swaddling, which involves wrapping a light blanket around the baby to keep him snug (see Figure 8-3). Swaddling also helps control the *Moro reflex*, which is when your little one seems to startle or jump out of his skin for no reason at all!

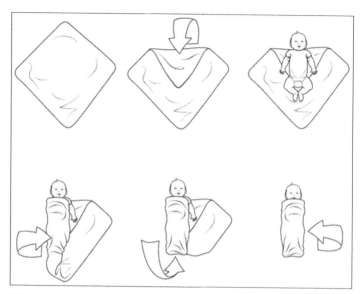

FIGURE 8-3: How to swaddle a baby.

Crying — you, your partner and the baby

At some stage, crying is bound to take place in your household. A healthy baby may cry for several hours per day (or more). Crying is your baby's way of telling you he's hungry, lonely, tired, in pain, gassy, too hot, or needs a nappy change. Sometimes he cries for no apparent reason at all.

Trying to figure out what the problem is while your baby howls can be stressful. Sometimes you may find yourself wanting to stop the noise whatever way you can. Crying can make you feel angry and frustrated, and you may want to lash out physically.

TIP

If you feel the crying is getting too much for you, put your baby in a safe place such as his bassinet or cot, and then take a few minutes to calm yourself outside. A very short but demanding exercise can help get rid of some excess adrenalin as well — so 'get down and give me 20'.

Whenever your baby starts crying, get into the habit of checking three things: is he hungry, has he got a dirty nappy, and is he comfortable and well (does he have a high temperature, are any signs of vomit evident, and are any other obvious signs of a health problem apparent)?

After you've checked your baby, do one (or all) of the following to try to calm and comfort your baby:

>> Burp him to help him bring up wind (if he's just had a feed).

>> Cuddle and sing to him in a calm soothing voice, or put on a playlist of gentle lullabies.

>> Give him a warm bath.

>> Put him down for a nap, he may just be tired (no kidding).

>> Put your baby in the car and go for a drive around the block (not the most environmentally friendly alternative, but sometimes driving's the one thing that works).

>> Switch on a household appliance that makes a monotonous sound, such as a hairdryer, vacuum cleaner or washing machine. Or download some 'white noise' sounds from the internet and play the noise to your baby.

>> Take him for a walk in the stroller or baby carrier (at any time of the day or night).

>> Try a gentle soothing massage.

REMEMBER

Sometimes your baby is upset and you can literally do nothing about it. The feeling that comes from not being able to control everything is horrible. But keep in mind that getting mad won't make things better. No baby ever looked at a cranky dad and thought, *Well, since you're so upset about things, I'll calm down for you.*

Under no circumstances should you ever hit, shake or lash out at your baby, regardless of how tired you are or how long the baby has been screaming.

Daddy time

Spending time with your baby doesn't have to be all work and no play. Every nappy change is an opportunity to have some fun with your little one.

Besides the usual chores and jobs you do with your baby, you can hang out together in other ways that are just good old-fashioned fun. Try these out for size:

>> **Bathe or shower together.** Bathing together can be a little nerve-racking at first. Make sure mum is standing by with a towel when you're ready to get out. Hold the soap — you don't want things to get slippery!

>> **Enjoy some tummy time.** Tummy time is where your baby lies on the floor on his stomach and tries to lift his head, which helps develop junior's neck, shoulder and core strength.

>> **Have a chat.** Babies coo from a few weeks old and delight in having their sounds repeated back to them.

>> **Read to your baby.** It's never too early to turn your baby onto reading. He can delight in the experience of being near you and seeing magical shapes and colours in the pictures.

>> **Sing to your baby.** You can sing numerous good songs to your baby, but you can always make up your own. And bub doesn't care if you can't hold a tune. He just adores you more for it.

>> **Take a trip to the park.** Your champ's a little too young for slides and flying foxes, but he loves sitting on your lap with you on the swing for a gentle swing back and forth. He also loves being outside and around other children.

Juggling Your Other Priorities

Before your baby came along, you were a partner, son, brother, friend, employee or boss and a member of your extended family. Now that bub has arrived and your priorities have changed, fitting in all those aspects of your life can be a struggle. You can not only jeopardise the relationships you have with people in your life by letting fatherhood take over everything, but also lose your relationship with yourself and find your own wellbeing at risk.

Making time for yourself

You don't stop being the person you were before bub came along. You still need to take care of yourself so you can be the best father — and partner and so on — you can be for a long time. Just as mums need time to themselves, dads deserve some time off too. Having a chat with your partner about continuing to fit in sport or time with mates is important.

Making time for yourself may make you feel a little guilty and can be tricky to manage, but you need to take care of yourself before you can take care of anyone else.

Looking after your partner

Some childcare organisations have a tendency to hammer the message 'baby comes first', which is, of course, important.

However, taking care of your baby can't be at the constant expense of your relationship. After all, if your relationship goes down the drain, a lot more trouble is ahead.

If you're the primary caregiver, you know what it means to look after a baby all day and sort out the household at the same time. Being primary caregiver is a lot of hard work, so get your partner to help out when she gets home. If you're the main provider, make sure you chip in and do whatever needs to be done when you get home. Yes, working all day and then helping out at home while looking after the baby is tough, but you can get through it. Looking after a baby and child does get easier over time — promise!

Above all, you and your partner need to have 'us' time and spend quality time together. You can do this by getting friends or family to look after the baby for a few hours while you go out, or even making a big deal out of a special occasion and celebrating at home when bub is asleep.

Here are some more ideas to keep your relationship alive and kicking:

>> Invite some friends (especially those you're both friends with) over to cook dinner for you (or with you). Yes, inviting people to cook you a meal is cheeky but most people are only too willing to help out. This way you two get to see your friends, have a classy meal and don't have to do any work!

>> Surprise each other with little gestures such as leaving messages, buying a little treat or present, or finding a movie you both will love.

>> Take a walk together with bub asleep in the pram. That way, the two of you can get some gentle exercise and spend time together.

We are family

Your newborn isn't just your pride and joy, but also the pride and joy of your entire extended family. Nothing is like having a child to help you realise what your own parents went through when you were a kid. They undoubtedly want to be part of your new child's life. So share the love!

DEALING WITH VISITORS

They say it takes a village to bring up a child. When your baby has arrived, you might realise that at least half of that village wants to drop in to check out the new addition to your family. Apart from your immediate family, expect to see neighbours you didn't know you had, uncles and aunts you haven't seen since you were a kid, old colleagues, acquaintances and, of course, all your and your partner's friends. Although you may want to show off your greatest creation, the demands of looking after a newborn (the sleep deprivation, the unfolded washing, the plates that are piling up everywhere) and your own anxiety about parenting don't make a great mix for entertaining. But you can turn a horde of visitors into an army of helpers with the following:

- Don't serve tea or coffee when visitors come over. Point them to the kettle — or the vacuum cleaner or washing machine.

- If someone rings and says they're coming over, get them to pick up any supplies you're too busy or exhausted to get from the supermarket yourself.

- Make the most of offers — people love to help and contribute in any way they can.

- Put a sign up on your front door with something like 'Parents and baby sleeping, please phone to let us know when you're coming over'. Screen calls — that's what voicemail is for.

- Don't be afraid to say 'no' when you just don't feel like having people over. People are generally quite understanding, especially if they have children themselves.

Having a lot of interaction with his grandparents, cousins and other close relatives is invaluable for your baby — the more love coming at him, the better. Having your baby feel comfortable and safe with family members also means having a lot of babysitters and extra pairs of hands when you or your partner are finding things tough. Interacting with different people also helps your baby develop his social skills and builds confidence.

Managing the work–life balance

Managing your commitments at work and your life outside paid employment is often a tricky one in this fast-paced society. Technology that allows you to work and be contactable 24 hours per day doesn't help you separate work from leisure time. Even before becoming a father, finding time to do the things you love may have been a stretch. Now you have the extra demands of a family, you may need to readdress your work–life balance and take some steps so you don't burn out.

In Australia, *flexitime*, or working more flexible hours, is becoming more accepted, especially for men. In some workplaces, you may be able to design your own hours, bank up hours worked to take days off in lieu, or add a no-overtime clause to your contract. And the opportunity for parental leave is increasing in many organisations, allowing you to savour these early days with baby. Take advantage of this if it's available. It's a good thing.

CHECK THE NET

To find out how to go about setting up flexible working hours and what rights you have, go to www.fairwork.gov.au and search 'flexible working arrangements'.

Sex

Having a little nooky is probably the last thing on mum's mind for a few weeks (or months) after birth and this can be rough on a new dad. The lack of lovin' isn't because you smell bad or have suddenly become repulsive. Blame it on the hormones, lack of sleep, leaky breasts and the time it takes to recover from birth.

Most doctors recommend waiting at least six weeks after birth before having sex. That's the length of time it takes for the uterus to get back to pre-baby size after a vaginal birth — and for your partner's body to recover from the labour.

Women who've had a rough labour and some kind of intervention such as ventouse or forceps should wait longer and may not want to resume intimate activities any earlier than 8 to 12 weeks after the birth. A tear or an episiotomy (refer to Chapter 7) can take six weeks or more to heal.

On top of that, your partner may not feel very sexy after going through the birth and seeing the look on your face as baby's head emerged. Your partner may feel self-conscious about her post-partum body. The right mental attitude is also required for having a sexy time. The memory of what birth felt like may last longer than the stitches, making the idea of sex unappealing. So you need to be a bit patient.

But things get better. Your lovely lady is really just taking time to heal, get her head around things and regain some of her mojo. It may take a few months, but her appetite for sex does return. So, in the meantime, continue to support and love her, and show intimate affection for her in other ways with massages, foot rubs and cuddles.

REMEMBER

When you're both ready to resume 'business time' again, take it slowly. Let your partner control the pace and position, so things are comfortable for her. You should be prepared to spend at least 40 minutes on foreplay, allowing her body plenty of time to prepare for intercourse. And check in consistently to be sure she's okay, particularly during penetration. Take things slow and steady, be gentle, and use plenty of high quality lube. And don't forget contraception. Breastfeeding preventing another pregnancy is a myth — and are you really ready for number two yet?

Chapter **9**

What Happens When

In an ideal world, I wouldn't be writing this chapter and you wouldn't be reading it. Your child should always be well, happy and carefree. But, unfortunately, life's not that simple. Children do get ill, they get hurt and, sometimes, tragically, they die.

When your child isn't well, you find yourself in uncomfortable, sometimes scary, territory. As a dad, you find that your baby's comfort and safety becomes all-consuming. And you often feel completely helpless as your tiny kiddo screams, wails and tries to communicate that, 'Yes, Dad, something's wrong with me.' It will throw you off balance, and leave you wondering how you're supposed to make it right. The trouble is that being a human means this is a reality of life. Sometimes illness is unavoidable, sometimes it isn't.

In this chapter, I show you ways to minimise the risk of illness, starting with pregnancy, and how to cope should serious illness strike. Lastly, I discuss disability and what support organisations exist to help you on your fatherhood journey with a child who has additional needs.

Avoiding Health Problems

What you put in your body plays a big part in your health. Make your home a smoke-free, drug-free environment. Reduce alcohol intake and be responsible if grog's around. If you're a little tipsy and you trip and fall while you're carrying bub, you'll never forgive yourself. And snoozing through a hangover while the baby feeds herself that two-day-old piece of icky food she found on the floor may have serious health consequences.

The following sections run through some more ways to ensure bub starts off on the front foot and as healthy as possible.

A healthy start to life

Doesn't every child deserve the best start in life you can possibly provide? Keeping mum tanked up with healthy food, lots of fresh air and exercise from when you first know you're going to be a dad goes a long way towards keeping your baby healthy in the long run.

REMEMBER

You're not the boss of your partner. Stay healthy yourself, create a healthy lifestyle, move and be active together, and watch the difference it makes for you and your soon-to-be family. Some research suggests that dads being active and healthy increases the likelihood that their kids will follow in their footsteps.

Avoiding risks during pregnancy

Creating a whole new person is an enormous task, and pregnancy can make a woman's body vulnerable to infection and conditions such as high blood pressure. Pregnancy can affect bones, teeth, blood flow, muscles and joints, and so much more. What goes into your partner's body — and how she uses her body — can be associated with the level of risk she and the baby experience during that 40 weeks of baby-growing.

REMEMBER

If your partner has any chronic health issues, such as diabetes or asthma, make sure both of you are happy with the way that your medical professional or health carer is monitoring the progress of the pregnancy. If not, find a health provider you are confident in.

These are some of the things your partner should be aware of during her pregnancy:

» **Alcohol:** Experts are unsure of what a 'safe' level of alcohol is for pregnant mums, so avoiding all alcohol is best. *Foetal alcohol syndrome* is caused by alcohol crossing the placenta and affecting the baby's developing brain, and it doesn't take heavy drinking to do the damage. Light drinking from time to time still poses a risk. Children with foetal alcohol syndrome can have problems with learning, concentration, hyperactivity and speech. For more information, check out www. nofasd.org.au. And consider taking a 'pregnant pause' from alcohol during pregnancy and breastfeeding — together. (Refer to Chapter 2 for more on making this commitment.)

» **Chickenpox:** When we were kids, chickenpox (also called varicella) is much like any other illness, and the only long-lasting effect of the disease may be a few pock scars. But in adults, chickenpox is a serious illness. If your partner gets chickenpox when she's pregnant, the virus can be transmitted to your growing baby. Though rare, the baby's development can be affected, causing limb deformities, mental retardation, or even miscarriage or stillbirth. If you haven't had chickenpox and you're planning to get pregnant, consider being vaccinated now.

» **Listeriosis:** Pregnant women are much more vulnerable to an infection from bacteria living in certain foods called *Listeria*. The infection, listeriosis, can be caused by eating deli meats, soft cheeses, unpasteurised milk, unwashed fruit and vegetables, raw meat, pâté, ready-made salads, smoked seafood and smoked shellfish. It's best if your partner avoids these foods while pregnant. Listeriosis can cause miscarriage and stillbirth.

» **Rubella (German measles):** If a pregnant woman contracts rubella, the virus can seriously harm the developing baby, including causing severe mental retardation and blindness. Most women are vaccinated against rubella as teenagers, but if your partner hasn't been vaccinated and you're planning to get pregnant, talk to your GP about being vaccinated now.

WARNING

Being vaccinated against rubella doesn't always guarantee lifetime immunity against the virus. Women planning pregnancy should have their immunity status checked.

>> **Smoking:** Pregnancy is a great time to quit smoking. Poisons from the smoke are passed to the baby through the placenta. Babies born to mothers who smoke are at risk of developing breathing problems, having a lower birth weight and being twice as likely to die from SIDS (*Sudden Infant Death Syndrome*, also known as cot death — see the section 'Reducing the risk of SUDI and SIDS', later in this chapter). However, quitting smoking is tough and not made much easier by having a preachy dad-to-be around, or one who is continuing to smoke himself. Instead, give your partner your wholehearted support and contact a helpline in your area, not just for your partner, but for both of you to quit smoking.

>> **Toxoplasmosis:** This is an infection that can be caused by a bacteria living in the guts of animals. The bacteria can be carried in raw meat and in cat poo, so pregnant women should avoid dealing with kitty litter boxes, and take care when gardening because cats may have used the soil for a toilet. Cook all meat thoroughly.

>> **Unprescribed drugs:** In case it needs to be said, the risk to mum and bub is significant if any other drugs are consumed during pregnancy (other than those prescribed by a suitably qualified medical practitioner and used as directed in relation to her pregnancy). Risks are present if your partner uses marijuana (or other drugs containing THC and cannabinoids), ecstasy (or other stimulant pills), cocaine, heroin, methamphetamine (ice), or any other illicit drugs.

>> **Vaping (e-cigarettes):** At the time of writing, insufficient studies are available to allow me to draw solid conclusions about the effects of vaping in pregnancy. However, I'm probably safe in saying that since e-cigarettes have any number of chemicals in them (often, though not always, including nicotine) any decision to vape during pregnancy would be risky. Even if your partner is trying to quit smoking and sees e-cigarettes as an alternative, my cautiously conservative advice is to stay away from vapes.

If you want to give up smoking, go to www.quit.org.au or phone their Quitline on 137 848.

CHECK THE NET

Encouraging breastfeeding

Encouraging and supporting breastfeeding in the first months of life boosts your baby's immunity and gives her the very best nutrition she needs to grow and thrive. Experts have highlighted that, for your baby, breastfeeding is associated with:

>> Better vision

>> Fewer cases of bacterial meningitis

>> Fewer colds and respiratory illnesses such as pneumonia and whooping cough

>> Fewer ear infections, especially those that damage hearing

>> Less diarrhoea, constipation and reflux

>> Less illness overall and less hospitalisation

>> Lower rates of infant mortality

>> Lower rates of Sudden Infant Death Syndrome (SIDS)

>> Stronger immune systems

And that's just getting started on the health benefits. Breast milk also contains substances that naturally soothe your little one. The positive health impacts have been found to extend even into adolescence.

For mum, breastfeeding is associated with faster weight loss (her body burns up to 500 calories a day just to keep creating that milk supply), improved post-pregnancy-related health (reduced post-partum bleeding and better uterine health), and reduced risk of postpartum depression. Breastfeeding releases feel-good hormones, helps with bonding, and builds trust between mum and bub.

I could go on for a while yet, but it's worth highlighting one more list of benefits to breastfeeding. Mums who can breastfeed are likely to experience:

>> Less cardiovascular disease

>> Less diabetes

>> Less endometriosis

>> Less osteoporosis with age

>> Lower risk of breast cancer

>> Lower risk of ovarian cancer

>> Lower risk of rheumatoid arthritis and lupus

Now that you've read all that, applying pressure to your partner to make sure she puts bubba on the boob might be tempting. Please don't. She already knows these benefits but, for a reasonable portion of women, breastfeeding isn't viable. These reasons include the following:

>> Breast reduction surgery

>> Depression or anxiety, or high stress

>> Insufficient milk supply

>> Medications that flow into breast milk and are bad for baby (such as antithyroid medication and some mood altering drugs — although this is an area that has a lot of mixed evidence)

>> Radiation therapy

>> Serious illness or other medical issues

Even if those just listed aren't the reason/s, your partner needs to be allowed to make her own decision. While it might be your baby, it is *her* body and *her* wellbeing.

REMEMBER

Breastfeeding can be difficult in the beginning, and your partner may be pretty exhausted and frustrated at times, so give her all the help you can.

Protecting against diseases

Having your child immunised against diseases such as whooping cough, meningitis and diphtheria protects her from these illnesses, which can cause death or serious long-term harm to a child. Talk to your child's GP about the right ages to be vaccinated.

Providing a violence-free home

Shaking your baby or hitting your young child may cause serious physical harm or death in extreme cases. The message is simple — never, ever, shake your baby, and consider smack-free discipline.

Beyond the physical harm shaking and hitting can cause, in the first years of your child's life she's learning to form a safe and secure attachment to you, her father, and this attachment plays a big part in how well she acts and forms relationships as an adult. If you're violent towards her, you're creating a serious risk of attachment challenges, trust issues and psychological difficulty when she is older. More immediate is the serious risk of harm. Adopt the policy that the only time you should place your hands on your child is to help, and never to hurt.

REMEMBER

If you're at the end of your tether and just feel like making your baby or child shut up, take a deep breath and count to ten, or leave her in a safe place and get some air for a minute. Stress is the distance between the situation in front of you and how well you think you can deal with that situation. Tell yourself you can handle it and see how much better you feel. She's a baby. She's acting like one. You're an adult. Act like one.

CHECK
THE NET

If you're often angry at your child, your partner or the situations you're in, it may be time to get help dealing with your emotions and anger. Check out Relationships Australia (www.relationships.org.au) which has links to services and courses in your state or territory.

Keeping accidents at bay

Keeping your child physically safe around your home, in the street and in your car is also really important. Here's a short checklist for things to keep in mind when you've got a baby in the house:

>> Keep your cups of tea and coffee (and any other hot drinks or food) well away from the baby. Your baby might accidentally touch them or knock them over (and so could you). Scalding is a serious health risk to babies and young children.

>> Whenever you leave your baby somewhere, make sure nothing can fall on top of her and she can't fall off anywhere. A soft blanket on the floor is the perfect place to keep your baby safe.

>> If you give your little champ a bottle feed, check the temperature of the formula or milk carefully. Using your mouth is the best temperature guide. Give your baby warm fluids only. If it feels hot to you, it's too hot for your baby.

Refer to Chapter 3 for car seat safety and Chapter 4 for safety around animals in the house.

Keeping up to date with household chores while looking after a small child can sometimes seem like brushing your teeth while you're simultaneously munching on Oreo biscuits. You wash and clean all the nappies, only to have junior need changing twice as often. Or she's suddenly power-spewing all over the place. You may have your hands full just tending to bub. But washing your hands after nappy changes, cleaning up spew or dealing with laundry is absolutely essential, and helps cut down the risk of bacterial infection from nappies and stomach bugs. If a global pandemic has taught us anything, it's good hand hygiene. So get the soap going consistently, count to 20 while you wash, and keep things clean.

You can also keep the following in mind:

>> Have a bottle of hand steriliser in your nappy bag.

>> Empty rubbish bins with disposable nappies and wipes in them regularly — at least once per day.

>> Wash toys regularly. Most plastic toys can be scrubbed in a basin, while soft toys can go in the washing machine.

>> Air your rooms regularly, to reduce the risk of respiratory infections caused by damp, dusty houses.

>> Keep baby's room at a temperature of 22 degrees Celsius, as recommended by the World Health Organization, and avoid any draughts. (And be sure you have enough clothing on your little one.)

>> Avoid tummy bugs by not reheating food for your child that's been in the fridge more than 24 hours. Cook fresh food, or food that's been safely frozen and thawed. If you need to keep food in the fridge, make sure it's covered; for example, with cling wrap.

WARNING

Don't store left over food in tins. The CSIRO explains that food stored in an open metal means 'tin and iron will dissolve from the can walls and the food may develop a metallic taste. Food containing high concentrations of tin can cause nausea, vomiting, diarrhoea, abdominal cramps, abdominal bloating, fever or headache.' Not what you want for your precious kiddo.

Reducing the risk of SUDI and SIDS

SUDI stands for *Sudden Unexplained Death of Infants*. In some cases, death is caused by smothering or some other known cause. SIDS is a type of SUDI and stands for *Sudden Infant Death Syndrome*, where the baby, for reasons unknown, stops breathing. Experts believe babies who have been around cigarette smoke are more at risk. SIDS used to be commonly known as 'cot death'.

Simple ways you can reduce your baby's risk of SUDI/SIDS include the following:

>> Keep your baby's environment smoke-free. If you both gave up smoking when your partner was pregnant, your home is now smoke-free. If you still need help with quitting the habit, call the Quit helpline in your area (refer to the section 'Avoiding risks during pregnancy', earlier in this chapter, for contact details).

>> Sleep your baby on her back, not on her side or front.

>> Keep your baby's cot or bassinet free from bumpers, duvets and doonas, cuddly toys and sheepskins that could smother her.

>> If you do share your bed with your baby (known as co-sleeping) only do so when neither you nor your partner has been drinking or is excessively tired to avoid the risk of rolling onto your baby. Co-sleeping is also safe only if you haven't been smoking, because exposure to smoke puts your baby at risk.

TIP

You can buy baskets that allow you to co-sleep with your child and prevent you rolling onto her or smothering her with a blanket. Check with your local baby supply store.

TIP

If you're worried about your baby's risk of SUDI or SIDS, consider buying an advanced baby monitor that constantly checks the baby's heartbeat and breathing. Check your local baby supply store for these monitors.

CHECK THE NET

To find out more about SUDI and SIDS, go to www.healthdirect.gov.au/sudden-infant-death-syndrome-sids. Also check out rednose.org.au and click on the Safe Sleeping icon.

Coping with Illness and Injury

Having a sick or injured baby or child is no fun. As well as feeling pretty darn terrible, your child may have trouble understanding what's wrong with her, not be able to communicate well with you about what's wrong, and be scared of the treatments she's receiving.

Spotting injury

The likelihood of your infant being injured is very small, and if it happens you or mum will probably be nearby. An immobile baby doesn't do much without a parent being nearby. But accidents do happen, and if you're not there when it does, it can be hard to know how to help.

A few pointers:

>> Never leave baby unattended on a chair, lounge, change-table, kitchen bench, car roof, or anything at all that she could roll off. Full stop. End of story. Your kiddo can't fall off the floor, so that's the only place she can be left unsupervised.

>> Never leave baby unattended in a bath, sink or any body of water. You have to be there.

>> Never leave baby close to anything that she can reach out, grab, and pull down on top of herself. Tablecloths, or perhaps that doily with a vase on top? Danger.

REMEMBER

If your little one is hurt, the most important thing is to stay calm yourself. Hitting panic stations results in poor decision-making. Remember — high emotions, low intelligence. Keep it level and balanced. You can think more clearly.

Here's a rundown on some unlikely, but possible, injury problems:

>> **Burns and scalds:** Run cold water on a burn for 20 minutes. If your child has scalded herself with hot liquid, take her wet clothes off because the heat in the liquid can continue to burn her skin. If material is sticking to the skin, don't try to take it off. If the burn is serious and you see redness and blistering, get someone to call an ambulance while you take

care of your child. Once you've finished pouring cold water over the area and if a trip to hospital isn't necessary, cover it with a clean cloth or tea towel and see your doctor. Your child is likely to be very cold from the cold water, so make sure she's dressed warmly.

>> **Concussion:** Babies have knocks and bumps regularly. Things can fall on them easily. A bump to the head can result in more than just a lump and bruise. Concussion is a temporary loss of brain function, from the brain banging against the skull. Your child may have hit her head so hard she lost consciousness, or has a headache, seems disoriented and may vomit repeatedly. Being irritable and sensitive to light can also be a sign of concussion. Take your child to the hospital immediately.

>> **Elbow and joint dislocation:** Some dads aren't aware of how delicate a baby is. In some ways your child is really robust. In other ways, things break or get damaged. And elbows and joints are one of those other ways. When you move your baby, never pull her up by the hand. Her wrist, elbow and shoulder aren't strong enough to cope with the strain of being pulled, and dislocation and even fracturing can occur. (One of my kids was the unfortunate recipient of this when I danced a little exuberantly with her and dislocated her elbow!) Always lift a baby with one arm underneath the bub, and the hand supporting the neck and shoulders. As your baby grows more strength, head support is less necessary. But even when they're older, swinging a toddler by her arms can cause serious injury.

>> **Squished fingers:** Your little one might reach out as you close a door or drawer. Hands and fingers can be easily crushed — or at least squished — so take care when closing anything with baby in reach.

>> **Swallowing foreign objects:** Your little one is guaranteed to pick things up and put them in her mouth. It's what babies do. Swallowed objects, choking, accidental poisoning, and even objects lodged in the ears and nose can cause serious injury and even death. Small batteries, a pin or needle, or even cat food (or, worse, cat litter) can all find their way into baby tummies or intestines. Keep stuff clear of your baby. Maintain a clean space. And watch what your bub is picking up and mouthing. And if you're worried, get medical help right away.

If in doubt about anything to do with your child's health, being safe rather than sorry is best, so visit your GP. For any of the following injuries, get yourself to the hospital quickly:

>> Anaphylactic shock from food allergy or bee sting, where the face or mouth swells and your child has trouble breathing

>> Bite from a snake, spider or another animal

>> Car accident

>> Convulsions

>> Eye injuries

>> Electric shocks

>> Swallowing of poisons, toxic material or prescription medicines that were not prescribed for your child

Emergency phone numbers

Make sure you have the emergency numbers for your state or territory handy:

>> **Ambulance:** 000 or 112 from a mobile.

>> **healthdirect (ACT, NSW, NT, SA, TAS, WA):** 1800 022 222 (24 hours, seven days per week).

>> **Nurse-on-call (VIC):** 1300 60 60 24 (24 hours, seven days per week).

>> **13 HEALTH (QLD):** 13 HEALTH or 13 43 25 84 (24 hours, seven days per week).

>> **Poisons Information Hotline:** 13 11 26 (24 hours, seven days per week).

>> **Parentline (NT and QLD only):** 1300 30 1300 (8.00 am to 10.00 pm, seven days per week) to talk about any concerns regarding parenting and children. This line is completely anonymous. Also check the website — www.parentline. com.au.

First aid kit

Keep a well-stocked first aid kit to deal with injuries. If you haven't got a first aid kit, check with your health care provider or ambulance service such as St Johns for sources where you can buy certified kits.

If you haven't done so, consider taking an infant and child first aid and CPR course. It can literally save the life of your child or the lives of others. If you haven't done a general CPR course for a while, getting a refresher by attending an infant and baby CPR course may also be a good idea.

Diagnosing a serious illness

The good news is that the worst illnesses most children cop are colds, the odd ear infection or a tummy bug. But some children have to cope with much worse. As an involved dad, you can probably spot the first signs of a serious illness, because you know your child inside out and can tell when something's not right. But now and then you might not notice a thing — until . . .

REMEMBER

If you miss the signs of illness in your child, don't beat yourself up. Unless you're a medical doctor, some signs are hard to spot. (And if you are a medical doctor, still be gentle to yourself. We all make mistakes now and then.)

Confirming your child has a chronic illness, such as asthma or diabetes, a genetic disorder or a disease such as cancer takes a doctor's diagnosis. Seeing your little child being admitted to hospital is stressful and anxiety-inducing, but fortunately lots of support is available.

If this kind of thing happens when your child is older, your child may be very frightened or blaming herself for the chaos her illness is causing in your lives. Try to be as open and honest with her as you can about her health and how you feel, and be available to answer any questions she puts to you.

CHECK
THE NET

The following organisations can help you in the event of your child being diagnosed with a serious illness. Don't be afraid to ask for help if you need it — think of the good it might do your child.

In Australia, you can contact the following:

>> Cancer Connections on 13 11 20 or www.cancerconnections.com.au

>> Diabetes Australia at www.diabetesaustralia.com.au and National Diabetes Services Scheme at www.ndss.com.au

>> National Asthma Council at www.nationalasthma.org.au

Help, My Child Has Additional Needs!

In the past, many people used words such as 'disabled' for children with additional needs. But these days, things have become more inclusive and oriented towards focusing on what people can do, rather than what they can't. If your child has additional needs, you'll probably become more sensitive to the way you speak about people with additional challenges or needs. In general, the use of terms such as 'handicapped', 'disabled', 'physically challenged' or 'special needs' is unhelpful and stigmatising. Instead, saying your child has some 'additional needs' is preferable.

Finding out that your child does have additional needs — whether physical or intellectual — can bring out all sorts of frustrations and disappointments. This is normal. Talk to a compassionate advisor about how you're feeling.

Imagining the hard road ahead of you can be devastating, and you may even blame yourself for whatever the problem is. But another way to look at your child's disability is as a way to motivate yourself to help your child develop in creative and unexpected ways. You can have moments of 'what if?' and occasional self-pity. But it's not about you. It's about your child, and helping her thrive.

Adjusting your expectations

When you first find out you're going to be a father, thinking of your child as a way to fix all the things that went wrong in your own life, or wanting your child to have more opportunities or career options than you did, is tempting. Perhaps you imagined your child becoming an astronaut, concert pianist or anything that she may dream of being.

So getting used to the idea that your blind child is never going to see the world, your face or her own children (unless amazing leaps forward occur in technology) may take some time. But then again, would Stevie Wonder have become the amazing artist he is if he wasn't blind? You never know what's in store for your offspring, which is really no different from the experience all other parents have.

Going into fatherhood, we also expect that our children grow up and one day leave home. Living an independent life may not be possible for children with a severe intellectual disability who need one-on-one care, 24 hours per day. This realisation can take quite a while to sink in, so cut yourself some slack and allow emotions and frustration to come and go. And find someone — a professional if necessary — to talk to. Talking your thoughts and emotions through can make a world of difference.

But incredible things can be said for accomplishing outcomes that are relevant to your child's world. The triumph of an autistic child who, with time, patience and the right support, is able to communicate her needs and ideas to a range of people, feels like a huge achievement. Kids with additional needs can teach us some of life's most valuable lessons — that life isn't always a competition, for example.

DISABLED IN ONE WAY — VERY ABLE IN OTHERS

Disabled is a misleading term. For one thing, it defines a person by what they're not able to do.

What do we most remember about Beethoven, Louis Braille, or Stephen Hawking? They've all achieved incredible things, far beyond what many folk without their challenges have done! The great composer Beethoven gradually went deaf, but was still able to create incredible music — eventually without any sense of hearing. Louis Braille was blinded by an accident as a young child and went on to create a way for the blind to read with their fingers. Stephen Hawking had a form of motor neurone disease called *amyotrophic lateral sclerosis* and was given only a few years to live when his condition was diagnosed in his early twenties in 1963. (He died in 2018 at age 76.) As the disease progressed, Hawking became wheelchair bound and needed a computer to communicate. Despite these breathtaking barriers, he produced groundbreaking work in the field of theoretical physics.

Other famous people who have shown the difficulties life threw their way don't stop success include actress Marlee Matlin, who went deaf from a childhood illness; Helen Keller, who proved being deaf, blind and mute couldn't stop her getting a university degree; and Dylan Alcott, who despite being born with a tumour wrapped around his spinal cord that left him a paraplegic, went on win multiple Grand Slams in singles tennis (among many other achievements).

And who's to say that your child won't be able to do what most experts think she can't do? You may find that your little one completely shatters your ideas of what it means to have additional needs and achieves much more than you ever imagined.

Finding help, assistance and resources

Knowing where to go to find assistance is a minefield. Start with your case worker, paediatrician or GP, the support organisations listed earlier in this chapter, and the following resources:

>> To access emotional, practical and financial support for carers of children with additional needs, go to www.carergateway. gov.au. To learn about support programs and payments, check out www.servicesaustralia.gov.au/caring-for-child-with-disability.

>> Association for Children with a Disability is an organisation based in Victoria, but their advice is universal: www.acd.org.au.

>> My Time supports parents of children with disabilities through forums and links to specific sites for disabilities: www.mytime.net.au.

>> The Raising Children Network, supported by the Australian Government and other agencies, has some great resources on bringing up a child with a disability: raisingchildren. net.au/disability.

>> Also see the health department in your state or territory for more information.

Chapter **10**
Finding Support

I n this chapter, I give you a helping hand to excel at your new role as dad by listing resources you can trust, and pointing you to organisations that provide useful information for dads. I also discuss accepting help from friends and family, and tell you everything you need to know about postnatal depression.

Help, I'm a Dad!

I wrote this book because I was once a new dad like you, starting out with mysterious new babies, wondering which way the nappy went on — and, no, I'm not actually kidding. It is tough at the start. Six kids later and all of that experience has become pretty handy. But starting out . . . whoa! I was clueless, and I needed a guide.

Being a dad is a scary, wonderful, adrenaline trip, and one many of us dads will judge our lives on. They say that no other success can compensate for failure in the home. This may seem like tough talk, but something inside us already kind of knows it. Chances are, you want a guide on the side to help you out of some tough spots here and there.

Asking for directions

Okay, I know — many men don't like asking for directions. That said, having a map or some cool navigation gadget does help. That's why I worked with Beyond Blue to create Dadvice — to provide helpful advice for brand new dads. You can find it at `healthyfamilies.beyondblue.org.au/pregnancy-and-new-parents/dadvice-for-new-dads`. Check out the videos, which include loads of funny conversations with comedians, dads having a drink, and experts with dadvice. Think of Dadvice as your map to fatherhood and this book as your journey planner. So you're off to a good start.

Finding trusted organisations and sources of information

In some ways, the people who know your baby best are you and your partner. You know what he likes and dislikes, what his little quirks are and when something doesn't seem right with him. And as hard as it can be to look elsewhere for answers, sometimes someone else may know what your baby needs more than you do.

For example, perhaps your baby is a bad sleeper during the day, is colicky or just doesn't take a bottle no matter how much you try. Maybe your little one is screaming and the only way you can keep him semi-contented is to walk with him, push him in the pram around the neighbourhood, and keep him upright. As adults, we're used to feeling like we're on top of most things; like we're pretty competent and capable. We know how to fix stuff. With babies and children, the situation is different. Many aspects of babyhood and childhood can't just be fixed. Things take time, expertise (sometimes not our own), and a whole truckload of compassion and humility — compassion for your baby and your partner, and humility for you because maybe you don't know as much as you thought you did. To overcome a particular issue, you may have to try lots of different approaches until you find one that fits.

Your first stop to finding these different approaches is your child health nurse. They have experience with all kinds of children, and can spend some time with your little one getting to know him and finding out what's going on. Another good place for information is the booklets and information you were given when your baby was born. Depending on where you live, your health service gives you a guide for basic baby and toddler care. These booklets often have good strategies for things like starting to feed your baby solid food, coping with crying and dealing with nappy rash, along with local services you can call in times of need. This book, too, has invaluable information on these topics.

Internet research

The internet's a pretty handy thing. With just a few keystrokes, you can search for anything your heart desires.

WARNING

Anyone can build a webpage, run a blog or comment in a forum, but that doesn't mean they have the expertise you're looking for. Gauge the quality of the information provided on websites by checking the organisation or individual who's responsible for it, their credentials, affiliation with recognised authorities and any ulterior motives they may have, such as financial, political, or religious reasons.

Once you're happy with the person or people providing the information and opinions, checking out forums where other dads are sharing their problems and offering solutions can be handy. Just don't take as gospel that everything they say is authoritative. And keep in mind that what works for one baby may not work for yours and vice versa.

CHECK THE NET

As a starting point, you can check the following sites for useful and trustworthy information:

>> **Dadvice** (search for it via Beyond Blue website, www. beyondblue.org.au, or go to healthyfamilies. beyondblue.org.au/pregnancy–and–new–parents/ dadvice–for–new–dads): Written by dads for dads, the site contains information about all aspects of fatherhood from newborns to teenagers, with a special emphasis on the timeframe covered in this book.

>> **Raising Children Network** (raisingchildren.net. au): This non-profit site is supported by the Australian Government, the Royal Children's Hospital in Melbourne and the Parenting Research Centre. The site has articles on all aspects of looking after kids, from changing a nappy to the tricky questions of spoiling a baby and spotting allergies. The site also offers a special section for dads.

>> **Happy Families** (www.happyfamilies.com.au): Okay, maybe I'm taking advantage of the fact that I've written this book . . . but my website is full of articles, videos and other resources to help dads navigate the challenges parenting throws our way.

WARNING

If your baby or child is sick, avoid diagnosing him by searching the internet. After phoning a health service, a real live GP is your first port of call should you be concerned about your baby's health.

Turning to friends, colleagues and family

When you're a new father, people are excited for you, and some may get a bit nostalgic for when their own children were little. They want to share with you their hard-won pieces of advice and may have an opinion on just about every aspect of looking after junior. Some of the advice may make sense to you; other gems are likely to seem bizarre. You just have to add each pearl of wisdom to your pile of approaches to try should you need to. Ultimately, you find out yourself whether something makes sense for your situation or not.

Turning to people who are close to you is an invaluable way to stay sane. If you're struggling, go hang out with a dad who's been through the wars himself. Looking at dads who've been through the crazy first weeks and months, and then come out the other side and want to have more kids, is a great way to get inspired and motivated for your own journey. You may at first think they've lost the plot but, really, these dads are no different from you. They've survived and, as many dads say, 'every day just gets better'. And no, they haven't joined some terrible cult and become brainwashed — they've just had children and, one way or another, that tends to have a big impact on everyone.

Not long from now, you may be the one sitting down with a new dad, hearing tips and advice flow forth from your own mouth!

TIP

Don't overlook the power of your own dad. If he was a positive influence in your life, go to him, tell him you want to go a great job, and listen. Learn. Ask him what he wishes he'd known, what he would do differently if it all started again, and what he thinks he completely nailed. If he was a lousy influence and completely blew it, consider what talking to him about your experiences might do. The conversation could blow up and go nowhere. If that happens, though, you haven't lost anything because the relationship was a mess already. But what if you went to him and gently said something like, 'Things didn't work out so well for us. I'd like to talk with you about what you'd do differently, what you've learned, and what I can do so I can break the cycle for me and my little one.' Perhaps closure, forgiveness, and new relationships might be possible. (But please enter a situation like this carefully. A wounded or manipulative, hurtful dad may not be good for anyone in your family.)

Starting a dad group

We all know a new dad or someone who's about to enter into the realm of fatherhood. Lots of dads meet at antenatal classes and keep in touch after that. Getting together to talk and share your experiences doesn't need to be a formal affair, with chairs in a circle and 'feelings'. It can be meeting for a beer while junior snoozes in his stroller, or a coffee at a cafe with the little ones clamouring over each other on the floor. Getting together can be just a gathering at the park or watching a cricket match. Finding new dads to join you should be easy, but if you're feeling a bit isolated, give your midwife or child health nurse a call to see if your carer has any dads living nearby on the books who you could catch up with.

TIP

An easy way to get together with other dads is to use the mum networks. Ask your partner about speaking to other mums about a dad get-together. Before you know it, a BBQ, picnic or stroller walk has been magically arranged and you can take it from there.

SAVOURING DADHOOD

Numerous studies have shown that if we truly want to be happy, we need to savour the great stuff in our lives. To savour means we amplify or extend a positive experience. How?

A great steak (or terrific seared tofu if you're a vegan) tastes so much better when you breathe in the aroma of that char-grilled finish, and when you then slowly place it on your tongue, close your eyes, and

(continued)

(continued)

feel those juices flow through your mouth. Slowing the experience right down and concentrating on every smell and every flavour magnifies the taste. If we're really, truly savouring that piece of food, we often groan in the bliss of the moment.

As a dad, you experience plenty of times when you don't feel like you have anything to savour. Being a dad is hard work and exhausting. And it will stretch you in ways you didn't know you could be stretched.

But being a dad is something you'll want to savour, especially while you have a newborn. When it comes to being a dad, the scariest part has nothing to do with poo explosions or having vomit on your shoulder — it's that it just goes so fast. You may not feel like the hours and days are moving fast when your baby isn't sleeping, your partner is exhausted, everyone's sick, and you wonder why you ever thought it was a good idea to have this kid. But time really does race by. Before you know it, your baby is crawling, then walking, then heading off to day care, and then big school. You'll look at your partner and say, 'Where did that time go?' So savour those moments. Take lots of photos. And relish every part of the breathtaking cuteness of your newborn baby.

We know when children have an actively engaged dad, they do better. At every level. Your little one needs you. But studies also show that dads who spend more time with their children also do better. It seems you need your little one just as much.

Male and Female Postnatal Depression

Feeling 'the blues' is one thing; being in a black hole is another. That's how some people describe postnatal depression (PND). The condition is associated with mothers for the most part, with an estimated 10 to 15 per cent of mothers suffering from postnatal depression. What's less well known is that 3 to 10 per cent of fathers can suffer from PND too.

While many men report feeling left out of their partners' lives as mothers deal with the constant needs of their babies and their own exhaustion, others feel overwhelmed by the demands of work and hectic situations at home. At worst, you may even have negative or guilty feelings about your baby and feel you're a bad father or partner.

Other contributing factors can include:

>> not being able to bond with your baby

>> attitudes towards fatherhood and masculinity — thinking you can't talk about how you're feeling or ask for support, or a fear that you'll be seen as a 'failure' if you're not coping

>> changes in your relationship with your partner, which can lead to feelings of resentment and exclusion

>> worries about extra responsibilities, financial burdens and managing the stress of work

Knowing about and recognising some of the signs of PND can assist you to seek help for yourself or someone else with PND. Some of the signs of PND to look for include

>> Anxiety or panic attacks

>> Feelings of hopelessness

>> Frequent crying spells

>> Loss of energy and appetite

>> Loss of enjoyment in everyday activities, and in your baby

>> Loss of sex drive

>> Mood swings

>> Problems sleeping even when baby is settled

>> Prolonged feelings of sadness and hopelessness, with nothing to look forward to

>> Suicidal thoughts

Every case is different. If you feel you or your partner may have PND, talk to each other about how you're feeling and see your GP.

If your partner has PND, supporting her may seem like a pretty impossible task and you may feel out of your depth. You can help in lots of ways. Try some of these ideas:

>> Arrange things so you can spend time together with your partner — alone. Regular 'us' time helps de-stress both of you and helps you to find and share some common ground again.

>> Let her talk while you listen, or involve a friend she feels comfortable talking to.

>> Take over more of the housework and baby care, and try to let her get some sleep. If you can't take on everything, call in some support from family and friends so you're not swamped as well.

>> Treat her in some way — for example, with a night at the movies, a massage voucher, a bunch of flowers or a special gift.

>> Visit your doctor and get professional guidance.

Postnatal depression in men, though not as common as PND in women, is just as serious. Admitting a problem exists is difficult. You may find the following helpful:

>> **Find support in your community:** In Australia, talk to PANDA (www.panda.org.au) on 1300 726 306 or Beyond Blue (www.beyondblue.org.au) on 1300 22 4636.

>> **Get some exercise:** Feeling fit and active can lift your mood. Around 30 minutes of daily activity is all you need to release mood-enhancing hormones.

>> **Talk to family and friends:** This step can be a biggie, but you're likely to be amazed at how keen people are to help. Chances are some of your mates have gone through the same thing.

>> **Talk to your doctor:** Your GP can offer you a range of options, including counselling and medication.

Postnatal depression is temporary, and you can find a way through it. If you feel lost, take stock and get some help.

Do you feel like screaming?

If everything's getting too much for you and you need time out, here's a tip. Take time out from your partner and baby, go into another room or leave the house for a bit and let it all hang out. Scream the room, house or street down if you want. This works wonders at releasing tension and you're likely to feel like a new dad. Doing a quick, high-energy exercise such as push-ups to release excess adrenaline can also be really useful. Listening to a baby crying is one of the most stressful things you can expose a human body to (nature's cunning way of making sure the off-spring is well looked after and gets priority treatment). So don't be surprised if the baby is stressing you out.

REMEMBER

All your baby wants to do is please you. You are a rock star in his world, you're the bee's knees. When things are getting tough, you're sleep deprived, damp nappies are hanging on the clothes rack, it's 2 am and bub won't settle, remember that your baby isn't crying for the hell of it.

Support organisations

For practical advice on fathering go to the Dadvice website (healthyfamilies.beyondblue.org.au/pregnancy-and-new-parents/dadvice-for-new-dads). Other good support places to start at include the following:

» Beyond Blue: 1300 224 636

» Lifeline: 13 11 14

» Mental health services in your state or territory: Go to www. healthdirect.gov.au/crisis-management for a list of crisis line numbers for your state or territory.

» Post and Antenatal Depression Association: www.panda. org.au or call 1300 726 306

» SANE Australia: 1800 187 263

» The Bub Hub: go to www.bubhub.com.au, click on the Support drop-down menu and then Perinatal Depression + Anxiety.

5

The Part of Tens

Work out some important ways to make your partner's life much more bearable — and even pleasurable — during pregnancy.

Understand how to improve your baby's and your family's wellbeing through being a connected dad, and creating more engagement and bonding with your baby and your partner.

Chapter **11**

Ten Ways to Improve Your Partner's Pregnancy

P regnancy looks easy when it's happening to someone else. As men, you don't have to endure what's going on in a pregnant woman's body 24/7 — and a lot is going on. Media depictions of pregnancy have led us to believe that a woman demurely throws up a few times, and then swells elegantly into a glowing, radiant Venus figure, à la Gal Gadot. Finally, birth is quick with a few deep breaths, some loud screams and — voila, a beautiful baby is here.

Not so. Read Chapters 3, 4 and 5 for what really happens when your partner is pregnant, and then help her get through the experience by trying a few of these tips.

Take Care of Your Lady

Growing a baby is hard work and takes quite a physical toll on a woman's body. Sure, some women climb mountains and run marathons up to the day they give birth, but those are exceptions rather than your average woman's pregnancy experience. For starters, morning sickness can be debilitating and, for some women, the morning sickness doesn't ease off until the pregnancy is over.

The tiredness and carrying of all that blood, fluid and an extra person around puts all sorts of strains on the female body. Look after your partner 24/7 if need be, especially if she's having a difficult pregnancy, and do all you can to make life easier for her. This may mean looking after the household for nine months all by yourself and, for sure, you're going to get sick of it. But, let's face it — would you prefer to squeeze a baby out of your body? So, man up and do whatever needs doing in the house. You can take it one step further and really pamper your mum-to-be by painting her toenails, giving her a foot rub or helping her rub oil onto her belly.

TIP

The best thing you can do for your pregnant partner is do the thinking. The cognitive load of running the house often falls to the woman in the partnership. Let her focus on the stuff that only she can do. Step up here and plan a few meals, organise the house, use the vacuum, and make a phone call or two to keep things moving.

Get On the Wagon

Your partner has to stay off alcohol, drugs, cigarettes, blue cheese, seafood and a whole lotta other stuff to keep that baby in there safe and sound. Seeing you downing a pint of beer and enough salami to sink a small ship could be enough to send her over the edge. Staying off alcohol and cigarettes, not to mention anything heavier you may be into, and eating what she can eat not only is better for you, but also sets a precedent for how you intend to live as a father. Plus, it shows you have a heart. So be considerate of her — doing so can only strengthen your relationship.

Give Your Partner Some 'Me' Time Every Now and Then

The prospect of becoming a mother, while really exciting for your partner, is also a daunting one, both mentally and physically. For most mothers, the first few months after birth end up being a

24-hour, seven-days-per-week job. They may have traded in their old life of meetings, schedules, work commitments and deadlines (which they may have varying degrees of sentimental attachment to) for the care of a tiny, helpless baby who they love. However, the role can be overwhelming.

During pregnancy, your partner is bound to have some trepidation about her new responsibility and how she's going to cope. Over the next few years, even perhaps until your child has left home, your partner's always going to have one eye on what she's doing and one eye on your child. So, in the months before this all kicks off, let her have some time that's just for her.

Be There for the Medical Stuff

Go along to all the medical appointments, scans and meetings with your midwife or obstetrician. Your partner wants you to be there to share in it. The first time you hear your baby's heartbeat through the Doppler or see the faint shadows of your baby moving and bouncing around in your partner's belly during an ultrasound scan, you'll be glad you came along.

REMEMBER

Although you're not carrying the baby right now, that tiny growing thing in there is your child, too. Your place is to know about how well your baby is developing, any potential health issues, and what options you as a couple have for welcoming your child into the world. Going to appointments also supports your partner because, in the event of any unwelcome news, you're there to help her.

Get With the Program

Start skilling-up on essential baby knowledge and skills. Mums-to-be love to see their partner getting excited about their new life as parents, and what better way to show your excitement than to throw yourself into the preparations? You have so much to learn about looking after a newborn baby and the months after that, so why not find out all you can about it now?

Ask your midwife, GP or obstetrician about antenatal classes in your area, and discuss which one you think would suit you and your partner best. Make never missing a class a priority, even in the face of work commitments. Let's face it — your work is there for a long time. Preparing for your first child happens only once in your life. And if your partner has any special preferences for learning about birth, practising for the birth, or doing whatever it takes to make things work better, be supportive. The investment of your time (and money) is worth it.

Go on a Babymoon

As a couple, now is the perfect time to take a relaxing and indulgent holiday somewhere. I'm not talking about backpacking through India or somewhere hot, with wild animals and tonnes of people, but somewhere low-key. Somewhere sun lounges and swimming pools are more common than office blocks, with great restaurants and shops to browse. Somewhere the two of you can just hang out, sleep late, read books and do whatever you want when you want . . . because those days are about to be kinda limited!

Be Excited about Becoming a Dad

Finding out you're going to be a dad can be a little daunting for some. And for others, well, you may have some reservations because of your own childhood, your financial situation, or the responsibility you're going to have. Your partner may also share some of those worries and concerns, but burying your head in the sand and pretending the baby's not going to happen doesn't help. Even if the impending change of lifestyle takes a while to sink in, you can definitely make the pregnancy experience more enjoyable for your partner if you show a bit of excitement about becoming a dad. Showing your partner that you're excited gets her excited and happy about becoming a mum. You want her to be happy and excited.

A lot of parenting is about attitude. The anecdote about dealing with picky eaters really sums this up. One father complains that his daughter is a terrible eater and doesn't eat anything unless it's got cheese on it. He's really stressed out about it and is pulling his hair out thinking of a solution. On the other hand, another father happily tells the first guy that his son is a terrific eater because, as long as it's got cheese on it, he eats anything. It's all about attitude.

Celebrate!

In a few months when the baby is born, you're going to be celebrating a new person's presence in your life. Not just any new person, but the person who is on this Earth because of you. That's pretty special! But the arrival does come with a price — temporary sleep deprivation and a restricted social life.

So make the most of your quiet nights and unlimited access to the outside world now! Take your partner for a flash dinner somewhere fancy, visit a special place together — do whatever spins your wheels as a couple.

One dad-to-be surprised his partner with a picnic lunch at the local zoo in the weeks before their baby was born. He'd even packed non-alcoholic sparkling wine to toast their health and a pillow for her to sit on. She spent some of her picnic time moving back and forth from the ladies, but the gesture was most appreciated.

Record That Beautiful Belly

In our great-grandmothers' and grandmothers' days, having a whole litter of children was common, and in some cases the pregnant belly was hidden away as if it were some kind of obscenity. These days, having more than three or four children is rare, and a woman having one to three children in her lifetime is more usual.

Celebrating the physical changes that take place during pregnancy (not the heartburn and piles, mind you), such as the voluptuous new shape of a pregnant belly and those plus-sized bosoms that you gotta love, is now common. Most pregnant women, while despising the weight they put on, love their bellies, so get out your camera from week one and get snapping. You laugh when you look back and see how your baby grew even before you got to meet your little champ.

TIP

Even better than snapping shots on your mobile, hire a professional photographer to take some photos of your partner's gorgeous shape. For some women, an album of professional photos helps her feel sexy and beautiful, and boosts her confidence.

Tell Her You Love Her

For many women, the hardest part of pregnancy is near the due date. Your partner may be having a difficult time getting comfortable at night and suffering from heartburn and piles. She may have stretch marks, and her legs and feet may be sausage-shaped. Your partner's tired all the time but can't sleep. She wants her body back but is frightened about how she's going to handle giving birth.

You, as your partner's great ally, her support and her rock, can show her that the changes she's experiencing only make you love her more by actually saying the words. She wants to know you still find her attractive and that she's still, despite everything going on in her body, the woman you fell in love with — not just because of the way she looks, but because of who she is — and that she's going to make a wonderful mother. Say it by using your words. Show it by helping her. And be it through selfless action.

Chapter **12**

Ten Ways Dads Build Baby's — and Family's — Wellbeing

I f you've made it this far into the book, you're planning on being an engaged, committed and present dad. The baby is either almost here or has already arrived. It's an exciting time, either way.

But you may have some nagging doubts. Being a first time dad is a bit like being a first-time driver. You know what all the buttons and pedals do. You know the wheel turns. But the first time you try to do it, you're probably going to be pretty clunky and clumsy. And you're almost certain to make a handful of mistakes.

Raising a child is a lot like learning to drive a car, or picking up a language or musical instrument. To get good at it, you have to make a lot of mistakes. Millions, perhaps. And yet it's the consistent effort applied over time — the practice — that leads to mastery.

Unfortunately, a lot of dads feel like once the baby is born, they're sidelined. They may feel they don't have much to do except earn the money, pay the bills, and try to be supportive while mum and bub bond. And now and then, mums go along with that because it's easier. They're the ones spending more time with the baby. They've had most of the practice with the nappies, the late nights, and dinner time (since dads don't breastfeed so well).

But plenty of dads want to be involved, positive fathers. And that's a good thing. Numerous studies show that dad creating a solid attachment bond with bub in the early days increases the wellbeing of the whole family. The research shows family functioning improves and relationship satisfaction between partners goes up (which is usually pretty good for sexual satisfaction too, so long as those first six weeks are over and your partner feels good about getting it going again).

REMEMBER

Involved dads influence more than just family function and relationship satisfaction. Researchers from the UK investigated dads' interactions with their three-month-old babies and found that by age two, the littlies with the most engaged and interactive dads were doing better on a range of cognitive tests than the ones whose dads were less 'there'. Mental development was enhanced by the presence or absence of an engaged father.

So in this chapter I outline ten things you can do to create more engagement and bonding with your newborn baby, and with your partner.

On your fatherhood journey, I wish you luck.

Get Skin to Skin

We already know that skin-to-skin contact is great for mum and your new baby. But dads can do it too — even if you're covered in manly chest hair. That physical contact releases bonding hormones in you, and makes you more crazy about your baby. If you're worried about messes, just keep their nappy on. You can still have skin-to-skin contact without total nakedness.

Work on Your Baby Talk

For decades, scientists have known that mums often speak in a more sing-song, high-pitched voice when talking to their babies. You may call it 'baby talk'. (We used to call it 'motherese', but these days we're more inclusive so we call it 'parentese'.) And for a lot of us guys, it can be a bit off-putting, and not many dads do it. Perhaps don't start off when you're in public, but have fun with your baby by trying some baby talk out. Watch their reaction. Talking to bub in this kind of sing-song voice often ups the engagement and delight your baby feels. And when that kiddo smiles at you, you'll have to hold yourself back from trying to eat him!

Sing

We all have different singing abilities, I know. But researchers have found that in the animal kingdom, singing is good for family life. A specific example: nightingales. Researchers have found that the better a male nightingale sings, the more supportive and protective he is of his family. The same research doesn't exist in humans, but the idea carries across regardless. When you sing to your little cherub, you'll look into their eyes, smile, connect and touch. You'll actually be supportive and protective. And you will bond when you do that.

Play

The world is teeming with data that shows that dads are uniquely more likely to play with their kids than mums. Of course, mums play. But dads do it more, they do it more naturally, and they tend to do it with more rough and tumble fun. You need to be really careful when your infant is new, but as she grows, this rough and tumble fun should become a staple part of your relationship. It helps with bonding, and it creates an understanding of risk, limits, consent and more. And it leads to endless giggles and laughter that you'll cherish for the rest of your life.

Feed

This is the bit where you can integrate all of your best attributes as dads. You can play, sing, talk in funny voices — and channel your very best choo-choo train or airplane to get that food into our child's mouth! And, yes, you can keep your cool when food ends up on the floor or all over you.

Bathe

When you spend time with a baby, time stands still and you get to completely immerse yourself in the moment. And perhaps one of the coolest bonding moments you can have every couple of days is bath time. True, you sometimes have to deal with unwanted bodily fluids or waste products prior to the bath. (Make sure you clean up their bum properly before bath time. No-one wants to bathe in their poop.) But once they're in that warm water, kicking their legs, splashing, and laughing their heads off while they smile up at you, you'll be a goner; completely smitten and lost in the moment.

Sleep

Everyone wants a good night's sleep. But babies aren't designed for that. They're supposed to wake up every few hours. It's just what they do. But with some clever design you can create a space for your baby to sleep close to you in your bedroom (or maybe in your bed if you're up for co-sleeping). Having their bassinet within arm's reach so you can hear their gentle breathing as they snooze creates that amazing calm that feels so good we don't really have words to describe it.

Pray

While a large percentage of Aussie blokes are ticking the 'no religion' box on the census (about 32 per cent in Australia), still a large percentage of the population claim a religious faith. If that's not you, this tip won't be so useful, but if it is, consider what praying with your little one close by can do for the bonds you feel toward her. When you ask God, the Universe — or whatever your faith directs you to pray to — for favours and goodness for your child, your heart feels like it grows ten sizes.

Be Still

Most of the tips in this chapter encourage you to be actively involved with your new baby in some small way. They demand you do something. This second-to-last idea goes entirely the opposite way. Sometimes, when you're with your baby, do nothing but stare. Soak it all up. Breathe in that brand new baby fragrance. Feel the softness of his hands as he grasps your pinky when you put it in his palm. Take in the perfection of his skin, the tiny lips, and the wide-open, trusting eyes. Engorge your eyes on the little tufts of hair on his head and the stilted, jerky movements he makes as he tries to make sense of his surroundings. And be still. Bask in the breathtaking miracle of the tiny wonder you've helped create and bring into the world. If you want to feel like a dad, sometimes it's best to stand in the majesty of the moment — even if it's in the lounge room while you're in your undies — and consider the potential of the little life in front of you.

Love Your Baby's Mum

Hopefully your relationship with your little baby's mumma is rock solid. Put her first. Be there for her. Support her. Think about how you can help her. In some strange way, this will build more bonding into your relationship with your baby.

But even if your relationship's not solid, take a step back and realise that this child is half you and half her. Acknowledge the good that's in her, because it has likely passed through to your child. You can't love the child without loving the part that she has played in your child's life right now.

Glossary

To help you understand the medical mumbo jumbo you may be exposed to during pregnancy or when visiting a paediatrician, I've compiled a list of the most commonly used terms.

active movement: Developing your child's fine and gross motor skills, cognitive skills and senses by doing things such as rolling on the floor, crawling, playing finger games and climbing.

active phase: A phase of the first stage of labour, in which contractions are increasingly painful because the cervix is nearly completely dilated and your partner's body is getting ready to start pushing your baby out.

amniocentesis: A test to check for genetic birth defects such as Down syndrome. The test involves inserting a large needle into the amniotic sac and drawing some amniotic fluid for testing. Amniocentesis is usually performed around 16 to 20 weeks into the pregnancy; see also *Down syndrome*.

amniotic fluid: Also called *liquor amnii*, this is the fluid that your baby floats around in, in the amniotic sac in the womb. When your partner's waters break, amniotic fluid is what comes out.

amniotic sac: The thin membrane that holds the *amniotic fluid*. When the 'waters break', the amniotic sac is what leaks fluid.

antenatal: Also known as prenatal, this is the period before the baby is born.

Apgar score: A score from one to ten given to a newborn baby at one and five minutes after birth to determine health and wellbeing.

artificial insemination (AI): Using donor sperm to fertilise a woman's egg inside the uterus.

assisted reproductive technologies: Using technologies such as *in vitro fertilisation (IVF)* and *artificial insemination (AI)* to get pregnant.

attachment parenting: A style of parenting in which close contact with the child is maintained at all times. Attachment parents co-sleep with their baby, breastfeed and carry their baby in a *sling* or *baby carrier* rather than a buggy or stroller.

baby carrier: A back or front pack in which you carry a baby or small child on the body. *Slings* are another form of baby carrier.

barrier cream: A cream you apply to a child's bottom and genitals to prevent nappy rash.

bassinet: A kind of mini cot or basket for newborns to sleep in.

birth canal: A term used to describe your partner's vagina during childbirth and labour.

birth centre: A specialised birthing unit run by midwives. Some birth centres are attached to a hospital, others aren't. Birth centres aren't available in all areas.

birth plan: A document in which you and your partner make clear how you prefer the birth of your child to go in the best case scenario. A birth plan should also include which forms of pain relief your partner is open to or would like available, whether or not you want to cut the umbilical cord, who you want to have in the room with you, and which kinds of intervention you're open to, if any.

bodysuit: A T-shirt that does up at the crotch with domes (clips) that's suitable for babies and young children.

Braxton Hicks contractions: The false contractions that many women experience in the weeks, days or hours leading up to real labour starting.

breech: When your baby is 'upside down', meaning the feet rather than the head are pointing down, ready for birth.

buggy: A large pram, usually with three or four wheels, that can be folded down either in half or lengthwise.

burping: The process of getting your baby to bring up wind by rubbing or patting the back.

caesarean: A baby born by caesarean is removed from the uterus through an incision in your partner's belly. Caesareans are performed when labour has been going on too long, or some condition in which the baby must be born immediately is apparent, or vaginal birth is too dangerous.

cervix: The opening between the uterus and vagina. The cervix is sealed shut during pregnancy and must widen far enough to let the baby through during labour.

colic: Persistent crying at certain times of the day, usually the early evening, for babies under three months. The cause of colic is unknown.

conjunctivitis: A highly contagious eye infection in which the linings of the eye are inflamed.

conscious fathering: Actively developing parenting skills and researching to understand why babies and children behave the way they do. Respond to your children by using these skills and knowledge, rather than with a reaction picked up from your parents or others.

controlled crying: A technique in which a crying baby is comforted at regular intervals in an effort to help the baby learn to fall asleep on her own.

cord prolapse: A rare event in which the umbilical cord blocks the baby from being born.

cradle cap: A type of dermatitis that causes flakes on the scalp in young babies, similar to dandruff in adults.

crowning: A term used to describe the baby's head showing in the birth canal, meaning birth is near.

cry-it-out: A technique in which a baby is left to cry and fall asleep on his own.

demand feeding: Feeding a baby when she shows hunger cues such as turning her head to search for a nipple, crying or sucking her fists.

dilation: A term used to describe the widening of the cervix ready for the baby to leave the uterus and enter the birth canal.

dizygotic twins: Twins from two different eggs, also known as fraternal twins. These twins don't share identical genetic material as identical twins do; see also *monozygotic twins*.

Doppler: An instrument that allows you to hear the baby's heart beating in the womb.

Down syndrome: A genetic disorder caused by an extra bit of chromosome being replicated in cell division very early after conception. Children with Down syndrome have varying degrees of mental and sometimes physical disability.

due date: The date your baby should arrive, though this is not for certain, because only 5 per cent of babies arrive on their due date. In Australia, the due date is technically called an EDC, or expected date of confinement.

elimination communication: Rather than nappies to catch poos and wees, parents watch their baby for signs they need to go to the toilet. The baby is then held over a potty.

embryo: What your unborn baby is from the time it implants into the uterine wall to about 8 to 12 weeks into the pregnancy.

endometrium: Lining of the uterus wall.

engaging: Engaging is when an unborn baby is getting in position for birth.

epidural: A pain relief method that involves a needle going into the spinal column with local anaesthetic. Epidurals are used in caesareans so that mum can stay awake while the baby is being born; see also *caesarean*.

episiotomy: Cutting the perineum to make the vaginal opening bigger during labour.

estrogen: Though estrogen's coursing through the bodies of both men and women, the hormone is found in much higher levels in women. Estrogen's known as the female sex hormone in the same way that testosterone is the male sex hormone. It's responsible for the growth of breasts and contributes to the menstrual cycle in women.

fallopian tubes: The tubes that connect the ovary with the uterus. An egg is often in one of the fallopian tubes and travels down the uterus to become an embryo.

fertilisation: When egg meets sperm, and the beginnings of a new child are formed.

foetal alcohol syndrome: Condition caused by a woman drinking alcohol in pregnancy. Foetal alcohol syndrome manifests itself as a number of intellectual and behavioural problems in the child.

foetal monitor: A device that monitors heartbeat, movement and contractions of the uterus to determine the unborn baby's wellbeing. Foetal monitors are used in antenatal check-ups in the early stages of labour.

foetus: What your unborn baby is called from the time it stops being an embryo, about 8 to 12 weeks into the pregnancy, until birth.

folic acid/folate: A vitamin that helps prevent neural tube defects such as spina bifida.

forceps: An instrument like a pair of tongs designed to help with the baby's birth, easing her out of the birth canal.

formula: A substance, primarily of milk powder, which is given to babies.

fundal height: Measurement of how far the uterus has progressed into the abdomen as your baby grows.

gas: A mix of nitrous oxide and oxygen that can be inhaled during labour as pain relief.

gestation: Another word for the time your baby spends in the womb. You hear your carer say things such as '30 weeks gestation', which means 30 weeks in the womb.

gestational diabetes: A form of diabetes that can be contracted during pregnancy. Your midwife, obstetrician or GP is on the lookout for it with tests throughout the pregnancy.

group B strep: A life-threatening bacterial infection in newborns.

hCG: Also known as *human chorionic gonadotropin*, a hormone made by the embryo to ensure its survival. Most pregnancy tests look for the presence of hCG.

homebirth: Your partner labours and gives birth at home rather than in a delivery suite at a hospital.

hyperemesis gravidarum: Extreme sickness, with continual nausea and vomiting, weight loss and dehydration.

in utero: Latin for 'in the womb'.

in vitro fertilisation (IVF): A technique in which a harvested egg is fertilised by sperm outside the womb.

induction: The process of artificially starting labour. Substances and procedures that mimic the body's natural hormones and actions are given to a pregnant woman to kickstart labour.

infant acne: A newborn baby's acne, caused by pregnancy hormones that are present in the baby's body.

intracytoplasmic sperm injection: A process in which a harvested egg is injected with sperm to ensure fertilisation outside the womb.

lactation consultant: A carer specially trained in breastfeeding who can give one-on-one advice and care in getting breastfeeding up and running. She can also provide support when breastfeeding's not going so well.

last menstrual period: The first day of your partner's period before getting pregnant is the date that the length of the pregnancy is calculated by. So even though you may have conceived your baby on the 15th day after your partner's period, your baby is already considered two weeks along or at two weeks *gestation*.

latent phase: The first phase of the first stage of labour, when the cervix is starting to dilate. Contractions shouldn't be too painful and can be managed with natural techniques such as heat packs and moving around.

***Listeria monocytogenes*:** Bacteria that live in some foods, such as soft cheese, cold meats and raw seafood. The illness *Listeria* infection causes, listeriosis, is dangerous to an unborn child and can cause miscarriage or stillbirth.

meconium: Thick, tar-like poos your baby does in the first few days of life.

midwife: A health professional who specialises in pregnancy, labour, birth and newborn care.

miscarriage: When an unborn child dies before 20 weeks gestation.

monozygotic twins: Twins who are formed when one fertilised egg splits. These twins are identical; see also *dizygotic twins*.

morning sickness: A side effect of pregnancy, usually in the first trimester, in which your partner feels nauseated and is hypersensitive to foods and smells.

Moro reflex: A reflex in which newborn babies seem to suddenly flinch in their sleep.

Moses basket: A basket that newborn babies can sleep in for the first few months of life.

multiple birth: A set of children born at one time, such as twins, triplets, or more.

nappy rash: A skin condition caused by the ammonia in wees and poos on your baby's bottom and genitals. Nappy rash is usually red, flat and quite sore.

neural tube defect: The neural tube is an embryo's developing central nervous system and it closes at around 15 to 28 days after conception. If the neural tube doesn't close, the condition can cause a birth defect such as spina bifida, where the spinal cord is not fully formed or not enclosed by the vertebrae.

nuchal fold test: An ultrasound scan done at about 12 weeks to scan for birth defects such as spina bifida by checking how the vertebrae are developing around the spinal cord.

obstetrician: A specialist in reproduction.

obstetrics: The arm of medicine to do with reproduction.

ovaries: A part of female anatomy where eggs are formed.

overdue: Any date past the baby's due date.

overtired: When your baby can't get to sleep and is too tired, he becomes overtired and more difficult to settle.

ovulation: When an egg is released from an ovary, ready for fertilisation from a sperm.

oxytocin: The hormone that causes your partner's uterus to contract, and is responsible for the let-down reflex when she's breastfeeding.

paediatrician: A doctor specialising in paediatrics, or care of children.

peritoneal cavity: the space within the abdomen that contains the intestines, the stomach and the liver, and is bound by thin membranes.

pethidine: A drug used commonly in labour, similar to morphine.

physical disability: A condition, disease or injury that prevents someone from undertaking normal day-to-day activities, such as getting dressed, eating or walking.

placenta: The lifeline between your baby and her mum, a dinner plate–sized gloop of blood and tissue that's attached to the uterine wall and absorbs nutrients and toxins from the mother. The placenta's connected to the baby by the umbilical cord, and is 'born' shortly after your baby.

placenta previa: When the placenta covers or is close to the cervix. It can cause bleeding, and your baby will have to be delivered by *caesarean*.

posterior: Where your baby is positioned head down but facing mum's abdomen, so baby's skull is against the back of your partner's pelvis.

postnatal: Also known as *post-partum*. The period after birth, usually one year.

postnatal depression (PND): A kind of mental illness after the birth of a child, usually in the early months. People with PND feel hopeless and detached from their baby.

postpartum: The period after your baby is born (usually a year). Also known as *postnatal*.

pre-eclampsia: A very serious condition that can occur during pregnancy, pre-eclampsia can cause stroke, organ failure and seizures in the pregnant woman, or cause the placenta to come away from the wall. Symptoms include high blood pressure and protein in urine, so your midwife, obstetrician or GP may test for these symptoms at each check-up.

premature: A baby born before 37 weeks.

primigravida: A Latin term for a woman who's pregnant for the first time.

progesterone: A pregnancy hormone that helps prepare tissue on the uterine wall for its special star, the egg, to implant. Throughout the pregnancy, progesterone helps get breasts ready for milk production and may be responsible for your partner's mood swings.

prolactin: The hormone that stimulates milk-making cells in the breast to produce milk.

prostaglandin: A substance that helps to make the cervix soft so that it can dilate and efface (or shorten) during labour.

reflux: A condition in which a young baby can't keep food in the stomach and brings up painful stomach acid in the throat.

ripening the cervix: When the cervix becomes soft and ready to dilate. Prostaglandins do this job.

round ligament pain: Pain endured by pregnant women as the pelvis widens.

rubella: Also known as German measles. If a pregnant woman contracts rubella, the virus can cause birth defects in her unborn child.

SAHD: Stay-at-home dad.

show: During pregnancy, material that makes up the 'show' has plugged up the cervix, keeping the uterus from infection. The show may come out and make an appearance in the days, or hours, leading up to your child's birth.

sleepsuit: An outfit with trousers and top in one piece, usually with long sleeves and legs.

sling: A piece of material or simple carrier that allows a baby or toddler to be carried around on a caregiver's body.

spill: When a baby has a milk feed, the baby may spill, or vomit, a small amount. Also known as posseting.

spinal block: An American term for an *epidural*, or spinal anaesthesia, during childbirth and labour.

stillbirth: When a child dies in utero after 20 weeks gestation, or dies in childbirth.

stroller: A pram that can be folded easily widthways, and can be carried by the handle with one hand. The child faces outwards.

Sudden Infant Death Syndrome (SIDS): When a baby dies during sleep for unknown reasons; also known as cot death.

Sudden Unexplained Death of Infants (SUDI): Can have a known cause, such as smothering, or be unexplained, such as in the case of Sudden Infant Death Syndrome (SIDS); also known as cot death.

swaddle: A term to describe wrapping a baby in a light cloth for sleeping, as well as the name of the cloth used to wrap the baby.

synapses: Connections in the brain.

Syntocinon: A synthetic version of oxytocin, a naturally occurring substance that triggers breastmilk let-down and contractions.

thrush: A fungal infection that babies can get on their bottoms and in their mouths.

toxoplasmosis: An infection caused by a bacteria that lives in the intestines of animals, particularly cats. Humans can also be infected by eating very rare meat. Pregnant women are particularly vulnerable to toxoplasmosis.

transition: A phase of labour between the cervix dilating (first stage) and pushing the baby out of the birth canal (second stage).

ultrasound scan: A handheld scanner run over your partner's belly to see inside. A picture appears on a TV screen nearby showing a grainy black and white image of your baby in the womb. Scans are used in the *nuchal fold test* to check for the possibility of birth defects, the development of your baby's body at 20 weeks or the presence of twins. If you like, you can also use an ultrasound scan to find out the baby's sex before the birth. 3D and even 4D scans are now available.

umbilical cord: The cord that connects the unborn child to the mother via the *placenta*.

uterine wall: The wall of the uterus, in which the fertilised egg nestles.

uterus: The organ in which an unborn child grows.

varicocele: Varicose veins in the scrotum that may lead to male infertility.

vena cava: The vena cava is the largest vein in the body and consists of two parts: the superior vena cava and the inferior vena cava. The superior vena cava carries blood from the head, neck, arms, and chest. The inferior vena cava carries blood from the legs, feet and organs in the abdomen and pelvis.

ventouse: An instrument with a suction cup to help baby be born.

vernix: A waxy coating that protects baby's skin in the womb.

vitamin K: A substance needed for the body's production of blood clotting agents. Some babies are at risk of a deficiency and can be given a dose at birth.

water birth: When your baby is born in a birthing pool or water.

wind: Air that becomes trapped in your baby's stomach. You need to get that air out by burping your baby by rubbing or patting his back. Wind is also the name given to air trapped in the stomach.

Index

About the Author

Dr Justin Coulson is the co-host and parenting expert on Channel 9's *Parental Guidance*, the founder of happyfamilies.com.au, and one of Australia's most trusted parenting experts.

He has helped innumerable families with his many books about raising children, his hundreds of media appearances and articles (including all of Australia's major news outlets, and even the *Washington Post* and the *New York Times*), and two viral videos that have been viewed a combined 80 million times!

Justin earned his PhD in psychology from the University of Wollongong. He and his wife, Kylie, have been married since the late 1990s and are the parents of six daughters.

Dedication

For every dad who wants to be great — and for the partners and children who love them.

Author Acknowledgments

A quick but important shout out to my 'Happy Families' team for their unqualified and unending support of the work I'm doing — even when writing a book throws our entire system off kilter. Evelynne, Caroline, Elizabeth, Abby, Jacqueline, Mim, Anna, Craig and JR: you make the magic happen. We change lives together and I'm so grateful.

Lucy Raymond first approached me with the idea to write this book. I loved Lucy's energy and vision. Sold! Except, even after my 'yes', I had to call Lucy and cancel. There was no way I had the capacity to pull this off. Lucy's tenacious commitment to the project — and her belief in me as the mouthpiece — is the only reason this book is in your hands right now. Thank you, Lucy. Charlotte Duff made me sound sharper, smarter and better than I really am. The editing process was supposed to be some scary, never-ending nightmare but Charlotte made it a dream, with witty insertions, real-life empathy and a perfectly aligned understanding of what I was trying to achieve. Charlotte, it was a professional highlight and you made it so easy. Much gratitude.

It's essential that I acknowledge the work completed by the authors of the first edition of this book. Stefan Korn, Scott Lancaster, and Eric Mooij laid the foundations for me to build on. Their first edition will have been helpful for so many dads over the years and it was a privilege to follow their lead with this updated and revised edition.

The rest of the team at Wiley has been a dream to work with. Mostly unsung heroes with whom I had little involvement, but who made the book a reality. It's amazing just how many people contribute their hearts and souls to putting a project like this together. To Ingrid Bond, Senior Editor for the coordination of all that is this book, Leigh McLennon, Publishing Editor responsible for project set up, cover and a host of other pieces of the puzzle, Renee and Marie-Anna for their marketing know-how (and patience with me), as well as Clare, Markus, George, Del and Kate, my appreciation. It is extraordinary how much complexity emerges in creating a book like this and getting it out into people's hands.

At a profound and deep level, I acknowledge Mum and Dad: Karen and Chris Coulson. They're the parents of me, twin sisters, my brother, and another set of twin sisters. Six kids in four births! Amazing! But it's really what they taught me about being a dad that I'm most grateful for. Dad's steady and constant presence has been the example I needed in my parenting. And Mum . . . well, if it wasn't for Mum, I couldn't have written so much of what I've written, particularly about labour. Mum, as a former childbirth educator, has assisted countless women to have their babies. But, more importantly, Mum has taught their husbands and partners how to support them through the miracle of childbirth in a way that connects them closer than they ever could have (or would have) connected otherwise. When you're reading about how a man can support his partner through labour, they're my words but Mum's wisdom (as well as some pretty handy science to add further weight and credibility to it). Dad, Mum: I love you, and thanks will never be enough, but it's all I've got. I hope your legacy can be absorbed through these pages to lift the lives of everyone who reads what's here.

And, lastly, eternal and never-ending gratitude to my own six daughters: Chanel, Abbie, Ella, Annie, Lilli and Emilie. And to my life partner, companion and wife, Kylie. I was able to learn the things in this book (thanks, Mum!) and be there for all six of these girls' births. And the warmth and connection — the belonging — that we have together stems from that foundation. I have no words to describe the depth of feeling and connection that I've felt because of those transcendent experiences in the birthing suites of Rockhampton's Martyr hospital (Chanel), Brisbane's Redlands hospital (Abbie, Ella and Annie), and Wollongong hospital (Lilli and Emilie).

Kylie, I will never understand what you went through to deliver these angels to our home. And I have even less chance of understanding how you did it. But I'll love you forever because of it. Thank you for making me our girls' Daddy.

Publisher's Acknowledgements

Some of the people who helped bring this book to market include the following:

Acquisitions, Editorial and Media Development

Project Editor: Tamilmani Varadharaj

Acquisitions Editor: Lucy Raymond

Editorial Manager: Ingrid Bond

Copy Editor: Charlotte Duff

Production

Proofreader: Susan Hobbs

Indexer: Estalita Slivoskey

Every effort has been made to trace the ownership of copyright material. Information that will enable the publisher to rectify any error or omission in subsequent editions will be welcome. In such cases, please contact the Permissions Section of John Wiley & Sons Australia, Ltd.

.

Printed and bound by CPI Group (UK) Ltd, Croydon, CR0 4YY

11/01/2023

03179266-0001